T0239424

Unleashing The Power of ChatGPT

A Real World Business Applications

Charles Waghmare

Apress®

Unleashing The Power of ChatGPT: A Real World Business Applications

Charles Waghmare
Mumbai, India

ISBN-13 (pbk): 979-8-8688-0031-3   ISBN-13 (electronic): 979-8-8688-0032-0
https://doi.org/10.1007/979-8-8688-0032-0

Copyright © 2023 by Charles Waghmare

This work is subject to copyright. All rights are reserved by the Publisher, whether the whole or part of the material is concerned, specifically the rights of translation, reprinting, reuse of illustrations, recitation, broadcasting, reproduction on microfilms or in any other physical way, and transmission or information storage and retrieval, electronic adaptation, computer software, or by similar or dissimilar methodology now known or hereafter developed.

Trademarked names, logos, and images may appear in this book. Rather than use a trademark symbol with every occurrence of a trademarked name, logo, or image we use the names, logos, and images only in an editorial fashion and to the benefit of the trademark owner, with no intention of infringement of the trademark.

The use in this publication of trade names, trademarks, service marks, and similar terms, even if they are not identified as such, is not to be taken as an expression of opinion as to whether or not they are subject to proprietary rights.

While the advice and information in this book are believed to be true and accurate at the date of publication, neither the authors nor the editors nor the publisher can accept any legal responsibility for any errors or omissions that may be made. The publisher makes no warranty, express or implied, with respect to the material contained herein.

Managing Director, Apress Media LLC: Welmoed Spahr
Acquisitions Editor: Smriti Srivastava
Development Editor: Laura Berendson
Coordinating Editor: Shaul Elson

Cover designed by eStudioCalamar

Cover image by pvproductions on freepik

Distributed to the book trade worldwide by Apress Media, LLC, 1 New York Plaza, New York, NY 10004, U.S.A. Phone 1-800-SPRINGER, fax (201) 348-4505, e-mail orders-ny@springer-sbm.com, or visit www.springeronline.com. Apress Media, LLC is a California LLC and the sole member (owner) is Springer Science + Business Media Finance Inc (SSBM Finance Inc). SSBM Finance Inc is a **Delaware** corporation.

For information on translations, please e-mail booktranslations@springernature.com; for reprint, paperback, or audio rights, please e-mail bookpermissions@springernature.com.

Apress titles may be purchased in bulk for academic, corporate, or promotional use. eBook versions and licenses are also available for most titles. For more information, reference our Print and eBook Bulk Sales web page at http://www.apress.com/bulk-sales.

Any source code or other supplementary material referenced by the author in this book is available to readers on GitHub (https://github.com/Apress). For more detailed information, please visit https://www.apress.com/gp/services/source-code.

Paper in this product is recyclable

"The Lord is my shepherd; I shall not want."

—Psalm 23:1

First, I would like to say thanks to Almighty Lord Jesus Christ for offering me yet another opportunity to write this book. I owe everything to Him. I take this opportunity to praise and glorify Him for all the wonderful things that He has been doing for all. God Bless.

This book was written few days after the death of my dearest mother, Late. Mrs. Kamala David Waghmare. I dedicate this book her and to my father, Mr. David Genu Waghmare—who both laid the foundation for my career. Without them I am nothing. I thank God for the best mom and dad.

I also dedicate this book to my adorable wife, Mrs. Priya Waghmare, for her love, encouragement, and care.

Table of Contents

About the Author ix

About the Technical Reviewer xi

Acknowledgments xiii

Chapter 1: Introduction to ChatGPT 1

Introduction to Artificial Intelligence 1

Significance of AI Chatbot Conversations in Business 6

Introduction to ChatGPT 8

    The Formation of ChatGPT 9

    The Technology Behind ChatGPT 10

    The ChatGPT Architecture 11

    The Future of ChatGPT 18

Practical Use Cases of ChatGPT in Business 19

    The Ethical Considerations of ChatGPT 22

Summary 26

Chapter 2: Understanding ChatGPT's Underlying Technology 27

Introduction 27

    ChatGPT for Machine Learning 28

    ChatGPT and Machine Learning 30

    Weak AI and Strong AI 31

    ChatGPT in Natural Language Processing 33

    Current Applications of ChatGPT for NLP Tasks 34

ChatGPT in Neural Networks 37

Technology Architecture of ChatGPT..41

Architecture of ChatGPT in Neural Networks..42

Summary...44

Chapter 3: Real-World Applications for ChatGPT................................45

Software Development...46

Customer Support 49

HR Operations 54

Travel and Tourism 56

Operations...59

Marketing..65

Sales 70

Content Creation 75

Translation 77

Summary...78

Chapter 4: Enhancing Business Communication with ChatGPT.........79

ChatGPT and AI: Unlocking Efficiency and Productivity............................79

Customer Support..80

Marketing Emails...80

Dealing with Global Suppliers 81

Internal Communication 82

Data Analysis and Insights 82

Automating Communication with ChatGPT 83

Automating Customer Service Using ChatGPT 84

Automating Internal Communication...84

Technology Developments in ChatGPT..85

Advantages and Disadvantages of Automating Business Communication
using ChatGPT 86

Advantages..86

Disadvantages 87

How ChatGPT Is Transforming Business Communication 88

Summary...92

Chapter 5: Implementing AI Conversation in Business 93

Why Integrate ChatGPT? 93

ChatGPT Integration Services 95

Use Cases in Various Industries 97

Healthcare 97

Real Estate 98

Finance...98

Education..98

Ecommerce...99

Tourism...99

HR...99

Entertainment...100

Customer Service Use Cases for ChatGPT 100

Strengths and Limitations of Using ChatGPT for Customer Service 102

Essential ChatGPT Prompts for Customer Service............................104

Simplifying the Tone of Voice...107

Asking Clients to Test New Features 108

Asking for a Customer Review 109

Summary...110

Chapter 6: Security and Ethical Considerations When Using ChatGPT 111

Introduction to Data Privacy and Security...111

Ethics When Using ChatGPT 115

Data and Privacy Concerns When Using ChatGPT 117

Information Risks in ChatGPT 119

Addressing Data Privacy Concerns in ChatGPT.......................................120

Deleting Your Chats on ChatGPT..123

Stopping ChatGPT from Saving Your Chats by Default 124

Regulations for ChatGPT 127

Best Practices and Safety Measures of ChatGPT.....................................128

Drafting a ChatGPT Usage Policy for Your Organization..................129

Security Risks Using ChatGPT..130

Malware...130

Phishing...131

Cybercrime 131

API Attacks 132

Summary..132

Index...133

About the Author

 **Charles Waghmare** Currently working with a leading Energy company since 2019 as a Business analyst in the Microsoft 365 space. Before that, he worked at Capgemini for eight years in various roles, including as a Viva Engage community manager and a manager of a Drupal-based enterprise knowledge management system. Capgemini Viva Engage network, one of the largest Viva Engage network was moderated by Charles.

Besides, he also developed a knowledge management platform for a global digital customer experience (DCX) organization using SharePoint Online to manage client references and knowledge assets related to artificial intelligence and customer experience (CX), and promoted Microsoft Azure chatbots to automate processes, develop proactive conversations with users, and create new use cases. Charles was awarded as "Most Engaging on Viva Engage" by Viva Engage Customer Network members in 2012. He is also a Viva Engage Community Manager Certified by Microsoft.

Charles also worked for ATOS (the erstwhile SIEMENS Information Systems Limited) for five years. During his tenure there, he was the community manager of SAP-based communities, where he utilized Technoweb 2.0, a Viva Engage-like platform, and on-premises SharePoint. Charles also served as the global rollout manager for a structured document management system built in on-premises SharePoint.

Charles loves reading motivational books. His favorite is *The Monk Who Sold His Ferrari*. Finally, he is a technology author of five books written on topics such as SharePoint Online, Azure Chatbots and Viva Engage.

About the Technical Reviewer

With nearly two decades of distinguished experience in the IT realm, **Subroto Singh** is currently a program architect at Microsoft. A visionary in Azure cloud and AI technologies, Subroto spearheads the design and deployment of innovative solutions tailored to meet the intricate needs of customers and partners. An adept trendspotter, Subroto is devoted to reshaping Microsoft's business blueprints, proposing scalable solutions, and championing transformative projects. Beyond the technical landscape, Subroto has an illustrious academic background, boasting a postgraduate program in artificial intelligence and machine learning from the Red McCombs School of Business at the University of Texas, Austin, and an MBA from the esteemed SP Jain School of Global Management, Dubai. As a luminary in cloud, architecture, and project management, Subroto's passion and expertise are reflected in numerous industry-recognized certifications, making him an invaluable asset to the field and an authority on generative AI.

As a fervent advocate for customers, Subroto's collaborative approach with stakeholders has been pivotal in refining project strategies and ensuring unparalleled customer contentment. This synergy extends to Microsoft's product engineering teams, where insights are shared to elevate the quality and breadth of Microsoft's technological offerings. Subroto's proficiency isn't just limited to architecture and deployment; he also excels in software project management, ITIL implementation, IT service management, and business consultation. His tenure in the health and retail industry domains was marked by groundbreaking achievements such as the pioneering integration of real-time Cerner/HL7 and the development of AI-supported personalized intensive care solutions. Throughout his illustrious career, Subroto has consistently demonstrated a knack for innovation, a commitment to excellence, and a relentless drive to propel the IT industry into its next chapter.

Acknowledgments

Thanks to Late. Alwin Fernandis, my beloved friend. He is not with us today, but his memories will exist forever.

Sridhar "Sri" Maheswar, supply chain consultant, NNIT: I thank you, my beloved friend, for your support.

Pravin Thorat, BU head at ATOS: I thank you for your prayers and good wishes.

My Church, the Salvation Army, and Matunga Corps: Thank you.

CHAPTER 1

Introduction to ChatGPT

In this chapter, we will introduce ChatGPT, explore the world of AI conversation, and discuss ChatGPT's role in the field. In addition, we will explore the history of ChatGPT, see practical examples of ChatGPT usage, and learn about ChatGPT's significance in the field of AI.

Introduction to Artificial Intelligence

The field of artificial intelligence (AI) is rapidly expanding and is focused on developing intelligent machines that can perform various tasks typically performed by humans. It enables computers to learn and adapt to new inputs by carrying out complex actions on their own. AI has gained immense popularity and is used in various sectors, such as healthcare and finance. The developments in this domain are the result of advances in hardware and computational power.

There are two types of AI.

- A *narrow AI* is one that can perform only specific tasks while failing to generalize beyond its domain. Some examples of this are Alexa and Siri, which are virtual assistants.

© Charles Waghmare 2023
C. Waghmare, *Unleashing The Power of ChatGPT*,
https://doi.org/10.1007/979-8-8688-0032-0_1

- *General AI* is a type of AI that's capable of performing various tasks and actions like humans do. Creating a general AI is a difficult and complex goal that researchers are continuing to work on.

Artificial intelligence is made up of various techniques and approaches. *Machine learning* is a subset of AI. It allows computers to learn by analyzing and making predictions on vast amounts of data. This type of machine learning is known as *deep learning*. It's best known for its ability to perform tasks such as speech and image recognition.

The field of *natural language processing* (NLP) is focused on developing AI systems that can understand and interpret human language. It's used in various applications such as translation and sentiment analysis. As AI continues to evolve, it presents both fascinating and daunting challenges. It can help revolutionize industries and improve our daily lives, while also raising ethical concerns about bias, privacy, and job displacement.

The field of artificial intelligence is a fascinating one, and it is quickly transforming the way we live. Whether you're interested in learning more about its applications or getting involved in its development, this chapter will provide you with a better understanding of how it could affect the future.

AI can be used in various sectors. There are a variety of practical applications in the field.

- AI-powered NLP is commonly used in virtual assistants such as Google Assistant and Alexa. It can analyze and respond to text and speech. It can also perform various other tasks, such as translation and sentiment analysis.

- Image and video analysis uses AI to recognize facial expressions, detect objects in photos, and moderate content on social media. In addition, it can be utilized in medical imaging and autonomous vehicles.

- AI is being used in online platforms to develop recommendation systems, which help users find the best content and products. Some examples of these include Amazon's and Netflix's recommendations.

- Medical diagnosis and treatment are assisted by AI in MRI and X-ray analysis, which can detect abnormalities in scans and provide cancer prognosis. It can also predict patient outcomes. Virtual health assistants and chatbots, which are powered by AI, are being used to provide helpful information and support.

- AI is utilized in the financial services industry for the detection and prevention of fraud, as well as for analyzing market trends.

- AI is an essential component for self-driving cars, as it enables them to navigate safely and recognize obstacles.

- AI has been utilized in video games to create more intelligent opponents, which can improve the gameplay experience. It can also be used in the creation of personalized recommendations for users on YouTube and Spotify.

- AI-powered robots are being used in the manufacturing industry to improve the efficiency and productivity of operations. In addition, they can perform predictive maintenance, which helps machines identify potential issues before they happen.

- Through the use of AI, marketers can now create customized marketing strategies based on their customers' purchase history and behavior.

- AI can be utilized in the monitoring and analysis of wildlife, as well as the optimization of energy consumption in different sectors to deal with and mitigate the effects of climate change.

- In the cybersecurity sector, AI is being utilized to swiftly respond to and detect cyber threats, such as phishing attempts and viruses.

- AI-powered educational tools can provide individualized attention and guidance, as well as assess learners' progress to tailor lessons accordingly.

We've seen a few examples of how AI is affecting our daily lives and industries. With the advancement of AI technology, we can expect more impactful and innovative applications in the future. AI can be beneficial for a wide range of industries and sectors.

For example, artificial intelligence can automate mundane and repetitive tasks, which can free up human resources to pursue more imaginative and complex endeavors. It can also boost efficiency and productivity in various processes. AI systems can accurately and quickly analyze vast amounts of information, allowing them to make more informed decisions and improve the efficiency of organizations. They can also identify trends and patterns in data, which can help them make better decisions.

AI can be used to customize the experiences of users based on their past actions and behaviors. This is particularly beneficial in areas such as entertainment and marketing, where recommendations tailored to individual consumers can improve engagement and satisfaction.

AI-powered assistants and chatbots can help enhance the customer experience by providing 24-hour assistance and promptly addressing inquiries. Such AI-driven interactions can result in shorter response times and better customer satisfaction.

AI can play a vital role in the diagnosis and treatment of medical conditions, such as cancer and diabetes, by providing more accurate and timely scans. It can also help with the discovery of new drugs and the development of personalized treatment plans.

AI can help predict the maintenance needs of industrial equipment and provide recommendations on how to improve the efficiency of systems and machinery. The development of drones and autonomous vehicles up to some extent is being driven by AI. These innovations can help improve the efficiency and safety of various sectors, such as transportation and logistics.

Artificial intelligence can aid in the detection of fraud and cybersecurity by identifying anomalies and patterns in vast datasets. This can be particularly useful in detecting financial transactions fraud.

The development of NLP has made it possible to improve the efficiency and user-friendliness of various services, such as translation and voice assistants.

AI technologies such as satellite imagery, drones, and machine learning algorithms can be utilized to analyze and monitor environmental data, aiding in addressing conservation efforts related to wildlife conservation, climate change, and resource management. AI-based educational tools can help personalize the learning experience for students by providing them with individualized content and paths.

Artificial intelligence such as Morpheus, a machine learning model, will detect and classify galaxies in deep space, helping map the earliest structures in the universe. AI can be used to stimulate economic growth by opening new lines of business, simplifying existing processes, and introducing novel enterprises.

Despite the positive effects of AI, it's still important to address its social and ethical concerns, such as privacy and algorithmic biases. Doing so can minimize the possible negative effects of its use.

Significance of AI Chatbot Conversations in Business

Today, customer support and engagement are vital factors that businesses need to consider succeeding. As a result, the rise of AI-powered chatbots has become a game-changing technology that enables them to deliver exceptional customer experiences. These computer programs are capable of learning and processing complex language and can be programmed to respond in a conversational manner.

AI-powered chatbots can help businesses improve their operational efficiency, customer service, and sales. They can also be used to interact with employees and customers in real time, all through a variety of channels.

Here are a few practical examples of how AI conversations can affect business operations:

- AI-powered chatbots can be used to answer questions and provide information about products, as well as help users with common issues. They can greatly reduce the load on human support agents and allow them to respond immediately to customers.

- AI can be used in sales and e-commerce operations to help customers make informed decisions and improve their experience. For instance, it can help them find the ideal products and guide them through the checkout process.

- Through conversations with AI, sales representatives can now qualify and hand over leads to potential buyers based on their specific criteria. This eliminates the need for manual lead generation and helps them focus on high-priority leads.

- AI-powered chatbots can help with appointment scheduling, allowing both the customer and the business to save time and reduce the likelihood of conflicts.

- AI conversations can be utilized to conduct surveys and collect feedback, which can be conducted in a more interactive and engaging manner. This enables organizations to gain valuable insight and improve their sentiment analysis.

- AI-enabled virtual assistants can be used in business settings to help with tasks and schedules, set reminders, and answer questions about company policies. They can also improve a person's overall productivity by handling various administrative responsibilities.

- Neural machine translation (NMT) is a method of AI translation that uses deep learning techniques and neural networks to translate the meaning of text and speech. Such AI-driven systems can also be utilized to provide real-time translation services, which makes it easier for companies to communicate with their partners and customers from varying linguistic backgrounds.

- Human resources and recruitment can benefit from the use of AI chatbots, which can help with the screening of candidates, provide information about the company culture, and ask relevant questions.

- New employees can be trained with personalized materials and instruction through the use of AI. This process can help them seamlessly integrate into the company and improve their knowledge retention.

- Interactive marketing platforms can leverage the use of AI-powered chatbots to engage consumers in games, quizzes, and competitions, leading to heightened engagement and participation levels.

- AI conversations can be integrated into software and mobile applications, allowing end users to get immediate assistance.

- AI-powered systems can also help employees follow proper procedures and follow the correct steps to comply with regulations.

In general, AI conversations in businesses can provide various practical benefits, such as enhanced customer experiences and efficiency. They can help organizations deliver better services, cut down on operational expenses, and gain a competitive edge because of their digital capabilities.

Introduction to ChatGPT

The term *generative pre-trained transformer* (GPT) refers to a type of computer program that's been trained on a vast amount of text. It can then be described as a language expert, which has been studying various books, websites, and articles about language to learn how people use it.

Through the training, GPT has the ability to perform various extraordinary tasks in language. For instance, it can generate answers that sound exactly like a person would say, and it can translate languages, answer questions, and have fun in conversations.

GPT can decipher context and produce relevant and meaningful answers. It is widely utilized in various applications, such as virtual assistants and chatbots. By analyzing and learning from data, it can improve its ability to comprehend and respond to varying languages.

Although GPT is very smart with language, it is still a computer program, and it doesn't feel or think like a person. With the help of GPT, computers can communicate in innovative ways.

The Formation of ChatGPT

The ChatGPT engine is based on the foundation of the GPT language models of OpenAI. There are many steps involved in developing this component. In 2018, OpenAI introduced the GPT language model series. The first model in this line of language models was released, and it demonstrated the capabilities of transformer-based systems for performing natural language processing.

The company continued to improve and refine the GPT models after the initial release of GPT-1. In 2019, it released GPT-2. This was a significant upgrade from the previous model, and it had more than a billion parameters.

After carefully considering the various risks and benefits associated with open source, OpenAI decided to make GPT-2 widely available to the public in November 2019. This marked a significant step in the evolution of large-scale AI models. GPT-2 was widely used and adopted by researchers and developers in various industries. It was able to perform various tasks such as text generation and language translation.

In 2020, OpenAI released GPT-3, which had 175 billion parameters. It performed better than its predecessors in almost all the tasks related to natural language processing. GPT-3's conversational variant, known as ChatGPT, was developed to show the model's chatbot capabilities. It let users interact with it as if they were chatting with a virtual assistant. As a research preview, this component was released to collect user feedback.

The company continues to improve and fine-tune GPT models through the feedback of users and research developments. OpenAI seeks to make the technology safer, more useful, and more robust.

The GPT series and ChatGPT have greatly contributed to the field of language processing, allowing developers to create advanced and more accessible applications. As the field of AI continues to develop, the development of these models will likely continue.

The Technology Behind ChatGPT

ChatGPT is a powerful language model that can be used to interact with machines. It's based on GPT-3 and GPT-4, and it was developed by OpenAI. This chatbot can provide responses and interact in a manner that's human. The ChatGPT is an intelligent and natural language processing chatbot that can converse with users in a conversational manner (as illustrated by Figure 1-1).

Figure 1-1. *ChatGPT can communicate with humans*

The GPT architecture of OpenAI powers ChatGPT, an AI assistant. It has been trained on a vast amount of textual data.

The following are some features of ChatGPT:

- The ChatGPT platform features a conversational style, and it can handle normal human communication.

- The ChatGPT platform will reject inappropriate requests from users.

- ChatGPT has the capability to understand several natural languages.

- It has self-learning attributes.

- ChatGPT has the capability to remember all previous communications from the end user.

- ChatGPT can programmed to develop new applications.

With ChatGPT, users can get in touch with relevant and timely answers to a wide range of questions and topics. Its data-driven learning system helps it analyze and improve its responses.

The latest version of OpenAI's GPT-4 is now available. It is the company's most advanced AI system. It has better problem-solving capabilities and general knowledge.

The ChatGPT Architecture

The ChatGPT language model has two main components: understanding and generation. The former is used to process the user's input and analyze the context. The latter is used to generate a coherent and contextually relevant response.

Through these components, ChatGPT can now engage in conversations that are human-like, utilizing the users' inputs to provide valuable responses and interactions.

Figure 1-2 represents a basic representation of ChatGPT's architecture, but it does not consider all the complex features that can be encountered in a live implementation.

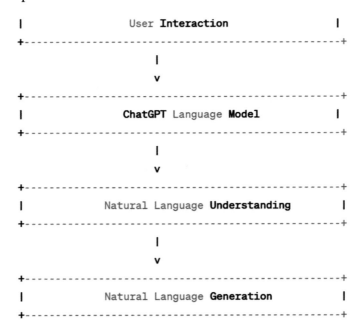

Figure 1-2. *CHATGPT architecture*

Figure 1-3, meanwhile, illustrates how ChatGPT works. A component that processes user input is known as a *language understanding component*. It can interpret the context and comprehend the intent behind the input.

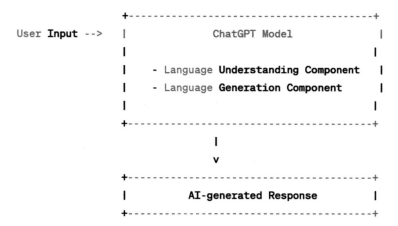

Figure 1-3. *ChatGPT at work*

The language generation component uses the knowledge from the previous stage to generate a response. It then produces meaningful and contextual language text.

The ChatGPT model produces an AI-generated response that is based on its comprehension of the user's input. It aims to mimic human speech and engage in a dialogue with the user.

Figure 1-4 is a basic representation of the architecture of ChatGPT, and actual implementations may call for more complex systems and components. This can introduce other challenges, such as computational overhead, but it might also lead to improved accuracy or richer output.

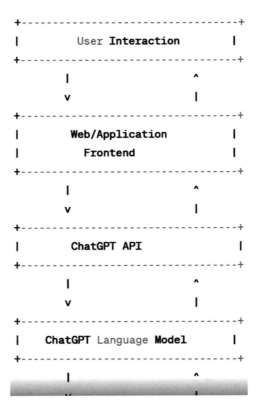

Figure 1-4. *ChatGPT deployment architecture*

This architecture allows a user to interact with a web or app front end using text input. The user's input is then sent to the model, which then processes it and returns a response.

In Figure 1-5, the ChatGPT architecture considers the multimodal context when it comes to user input, which can include videos, images, and other forms of data. This provides the AI model with additional information when it comes to producing a response.

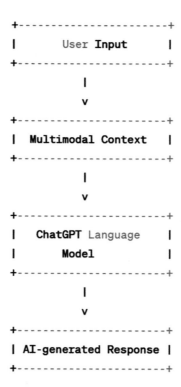

Figure 1-5. *ChatGPT multimodal architecture*

We will now explore ChatGPT workflow architecture, which will help us to deploy ChatGPT in a business context. We will explore ChatGPT training workflow architecture (see Figure 1-6) and ChatGPT interference architecture (see Figure 1-7).

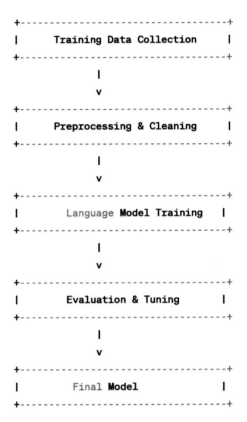

Figure 1-6. *ChatGPT training workflow*

As shown in Figure 1-6, the training data collection process begins by gathering an extensive amount of textual information from various sources. This includes books, websites, and articles. The training data is thoroughly cleaned and preprocessed to remove noise and make it suitable for training.

The language model is then trained using the preprocessed data, which is done through a transformer-based approach. The model is subjected to several iterations to improve its performance.

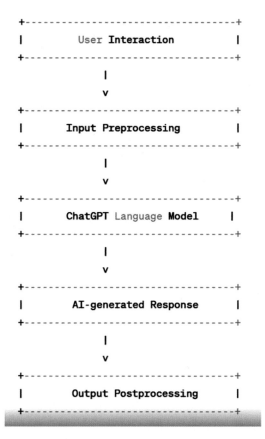

Figure 1-7. *ChatGPT architecture in interference workflow*

The model is evaluated on various tasks and benchmarks to measure its effectiveness. If the results of the tests are not satisfactory, the model is tuned. The ChatGPT final model is released after the successful completion of training and evaluation.

The next architecture we will discuss is the ChatGPT interference workflow architecture. ChatGPT users first interact with the platform and provide input in the form of speech or text.

The user's input may be preprocessed, which can involve sentence splitting and tokenization. These steps are part of the linguistic process that's used to prepare the language model's input. The ChatGPT language model takes in the preprocessed input and processes it before generating a response.

An AI-generated response is generated by the language model after analyzing the inputs it has received and the context it learns from the training data. Response output goes through postprocessing, which involves formatting and detokenization, to make it suitable for presentation.

The ChatGPT model's inference and training processes (see Figure 1-7) are laid out in these workflows. They can be more complex in live implementations, and they can be customized to meet specific requirements.

The Future of ChatGPT

The development of ChatGPT's language comprehension capabilities is one of the most important factors that will affect its future. Although models such as GPT-3 have already shown impressive capabilities, there is still room for improvement.

In the future, ChatGPT is expected to be able to provide users with more personalized interactions. This could include being able to learn from past conversations and tailoring responses based on the users' specific preferences. In terms of its ability to comprehend complex conversations, ChatGPT is expected to grow in leaps and bounds in the future. It may be capable of asking clarifying questions and handling more intricate discussions.

Although ChatGPT currently focuses on text-based conversations, it is expected to expand its horizons in the future and add other forms of input, such as speech or images, to create more immersive and varied encounters. As the technology matures, it is expected that ChatGPT will find its way into various domains and industries. For instance, it is expected to be adopted in education, healthcare, and creative content generation.

Future versions of ChatGPT may be integrated seamlessly into various platforms and applications. This would allow developers and companies to easily implement conversational AI capabilities in their products. Although GPT-3 and other large models can be powerful, they require a considerable number of computational resources to perform well. In the future, developments will focus on creating smaller and more efficient models that can be easily deployed on various devices.

As the field of conversational AI continues to expand, the need for ethical considerations will rise. This trend will also affect the development of AI models, such as ChatGPT. Developers must ensure that the models they create are ethical. The development of ChatGPT will be influenced by the ongoing research and collaboration within the AI community. Organizations such as OpenAI will likely continue accepting feedback and making improvements based on the experiences of their users. The development of AI technology opens new possibilities for chatbots and conversational AI. With that in mind, it's crucial to ensure ethical concerns and biases are addressed to uphold the positive impact of AI in society.

Practical Use Cases of ChatGPT in Business

As companies expand their operations and improve their customer service in today's digital era, they are turning to AI-powered language models to enhance their efficiency and deliver individualized experiences. One of these is ChatGPT. This versatile AI can be used to interact with users through a variety of natural language processing techniques.

ChatGPT is utilized in various industries and is a game-changing technology. It enables companies to improve customer support, generate leads, and streamline internal processes. With the help of ChatGPT, organizations can create intelligent and engaging conversations with their employees and customers. The following are some applications:

- Integrating ChatGPT into applications and websites can offer instant assistance to customers. This feature can handle various common inquiries and provide helpful product information, helping to enhance client satisfaction and minimize support costs.

- ChatGPT-enabled chatbots can be used to generate leads, help with the sales process, and answer FAQs. It can also increase the likelihood of conversions and provide recommendations based on the inquiries that it receives.

- With ChatGPT, marketers and content creators can easily create social media posts, articles, and descriptions for their products. It can also help them brainstorm ideas and provide relevant data.

- With ChatGPT-enabled virtual assistants, staff members can get more done by scheduling meetings, handling internal inquiries, and managing their calendars. This can result in improved productivity and streamlined operations.

- Integrating ChatGPT into translation platforms lets firms offer translation services in real time, especially when dealing with multilingual consumers.

- In the recruitment and HR departments, ChatGPT may be utilized to screen candidates, handle job-related inquiries, and help with the hiring process. This streamlines procedures and enhances workflow.

- In marketing campaigns, companies can integrate ChatGPT into interactive games, quizzes, and personalized recommendations to encourage users to take part in the brand's activities and increase their engagement.

- Virtual tutors that are powered by ChatGPT can be utilized in educational institutions to provide one-on-one assistance, clarify student inquiries, and offer individualized learning opportunities.

- In the healthcare industry, ChatGPT may be utilized to handle nonemergency medical inquiries and provide answers to patients' questions, alleviating the burden on overworked practitioners.

- In language learning applications, ChatGPT can be used to simulate conversations, aiding learners in improving their ability to speak another language.

- In the real estate sector, ChatGPT can be utilized to handle property inquiries, arrange property visits, and assist with the start of the sales process.

- In the hospitality industry, ChatGPT could be utilized to help with reservations, provide information about locations, and answer questions about travel.

- These are just a couple of examples demonstrating how ChatGPT could potentially be integrated into a company's operations to improve the customer experience, boost productivity, and encourage more collaborative and interactive interactions. The technology's evolution may lead to even more innovative use cases in the future.

The Ethical Considerations of ChatGPT

One of the main ethical concerns that users should be aware of with regard to using AI language models is the possibility for discrimination in their responses. This issue can arise because of the large datasets that these models learn from, as well as the existing prejudices in society. Developers must take the necessary steps to identify and mitigate this issue.

Interactions through ChatGPT can involve the transmission of sensitive data. Developers and companies must take the necessary steps to ensure that the information they collect is protected from unauthorized access. This can be achieved using encryption and anonymization methods.

ChatGPT and other AI models are often regarded as black boxes, which makes it hard for users to understand how they respond to certain questions. Having clear explanations and transparency about the decisions made by these models is important to build trust and make users aware of the limitations of the AI.

Users must be aware that they are conversing with an AI, and they should be informed of its nature. Providing sufficient disclosure of the AI's behavior is crucial to secure their consent. Clear communication fosters trust and prevents deception.

Businesses and developers should take into account the possible effects of ChatGPT on various applications. They must avoid exploitative or harmful use scenarios to stop manipulation, misinformation, or harassment.

AI models can make offensive or harmful content. Developers and companies must implement mechanisms and filters to identify and prevent such content from being created.

AI models must be conceptualized with values that conform to human rights, ethical principles, and societal norms. When creating responsible AI systems, consideration should be extended to society's wider implications. The implementation of safety features and protective barriers in AI models is crucial to prevent their unintentional or malicious use. The monitoring and auditing of their behavior can help determine and address any harmful outputs.

Developers must actively combat the misuse of AI models, such as ChatGPT. They should also develop clear guidelines on how these models should be used and what their consequences should be. The fostering of collaboration among policymakers, academics, and industry professionals promotes ethical conduct and establishes best practices for developing AI models.

While there is immense potential for AI models, such as ChatGPT, they also have ethical responsibilities.

- Developers and users should consider the various benefits of such systems while ensuring that they are used in a responsible manner.

- ChatGPT should have the necessary tools to filter inappropriate and offensive content. This is especially important when the platform interacts with users, as it has to maintain community standards and avoid promoting violence, hate speech, or other such behavior.

- As AI models become more sophisticated, they have the potential to influence people's opinions and decisions. To prevent this, developers should make sure that the tools remain useful and do not manipulate or trick users.

- Interactions with AI should be age-appropriate, and the platform should be able to provide content that's appropriate for everyone. Developers should also implement measures to limit the information that the AI collects and ensure that it complies with applicable laws.

- Developers should ensure that ChatGPT does not spread false information or misinformation. It should construct a model that can provide factual data and reject content that encourages the dissemination of disinformation.

- AI interactions have to be cognizant of the emotional well-being of users, especially those who are suffering from mental health issues. Developers must implement safeguards to recognize signs of distress and offer appropriate referrals.

- Developers must also work on mitigating the effects of discrimination and stereotypes in the responses of ChatGPT. This can be achieved through techniques such as careful dataset curation and adversarial training.

- Users should have the necessary consent and ownership to have their data used and collected. Companies must be transparent about how their data is being used as they interact with ChatGPT, and this should be done through a transparent process.

- Developers should prevent the exploitation of ChatGPT for any purpose, such as deceiving users or producing fake reviews. By implementing checks, they can maintain the integrity of the data that the AI generates.

- Users should have clear consent and ownership mechanisms and the ability to have their data collected and used. Companies should be up front about how their data is being utilized and stored by ChatGPT.

- Developers should not exploit ChatGPT for any purpose, such as producing fake reviews or distributing misleading content. By implementing checks, they can maintain the integrity of the data that the AI generates.

- As the field of artificial intelligence continues to expand, developers must take necessary steps to prevent the exploitation of AI-generated content for malicious purposes.

- Companies must regularly monitor the output of ChatGPT and collect user feedback to identify issues and improve its performance. Organizations should also have channels for individuals to report problematic content or interactions created by the chatbot.

- Being able to interpret the data that the AI produces is very important for developers, especially when it comes to handling sensitive situations such as medical advice.

- The interactions created by AI systems can have unexpected consequences. These can include causing harm or reinforcing stereotypes. Having regular audits and feedback from users can help identify these issues and implement fixes.

- As the number of AI models continues to rise, understanding their societal effects is becoming more important. To identify possible advantages and risks, organizations should conduct studies and assessments.

Collaborate with stakeholders and policymakers to develop regulations and guidelines on the appropriate usage of AI models, such as ChatGPT. These guidelines can help developers and companies promote the responsible use of ChatGPT. Doing so can help ensure that the technology contributes positively to society while also minimizing possible risks.

Summary

This chapter introduced AI and ChatGPT. It also covered ChatGPT's business applications. In the upcoming chapters, we will focus on the business relevance of ChatGPT, Gain understanding of ChatGPT technology, discover application of ChatGPT in real world, enhancing Business Communication with ChatGPT, Implementing AI Conversation in Business, and checkout ethical consideration whilst using ChatGPT.

CHAPTER 2

Understanding ChatGPT's Underlying Technology

In the previous chapter, you were introduced to ChatGPT. You saw practical examples of how to use ChatGPT, learned about its history, and explored the significance of AI conversation. In this chapter, you will gain a historical understanding of ChatGPT's underlying technology, including the technological aspects of machine learning algorithms, natural language processing, and neural networks.

Introduction

ChatGPT is a type of generative AI that lets users interact with text created by the AI. Like an automated chat system, ChatGPT provides people with a way to ask questions or get clarifications. The concept of a generative pre-trained transformer (GPT) refers to how ChatGPT formulates and processes responses. It uses a combination of human feedback and machine learning to improve its performance.

© Charles Waghmare 2023
C. Waghmare, *Unleashing The Power of ChatGPT*,
https://doi.org/10.1007/979-8-8688-0032-0_2

Founded in 2015, OpenAI developed ChatGPT. It was cofounded by Sam Altman and officially launched in November 2022. The company is backed by various investors, such as Microsoft. In addition, it developed Dall-E, a text-to-art generator.

ChatGPT uses a GPT, which is designed to find patterns in data sequences. GPT-3 is a large language model and a neural network learning framework.

ChatGPT for Machine Learning

ChatGPT is a revolutionary language processing model that uses machine learning techniques. It represents a significant advance in AI. The model is built on the GPT-3.5 framework, which is a type of neural network designed to recognize and generate human-like texts.

ChatGPT is designed to provide users with a more accurate and contextual understanding of their conversations. It accomplishes this through its use of a deep learning algorithm that has been extensively trained on a vast collection of text from the Internet. This pre-training ensures that ChatGPT can handle the various nuances of human language.

With the help of its fine-tuning process, ChatGPT can be customized to perform specific tasks or applications. This allows it to excel in certain fields, such as customer support, healthcare, and finance. It is a versatile tool that can be used in different industries.

ChatGPT's algorithms are built on deep neural networks that are rooted in the transformer architecture, which is a well-suited framework for processing sequential data. These algorithms are composed of multiple feedforward networks and attention mechanisms, which enable the model to perform effective and contextual language processing.

Through reinforcement learning, the ChatGPT model can learn and improve through user-generated content. Its fine-tuning phase also allows it to respond to feedback in real life to enhance its capabilities in providing helpful and accurate information.

The development of the ChatGPT algorithms marks a significant advance in the field of conversational AI. It can revolutionize various applications, such as virtual assistants and content generation. It can comprehend and produce human-like texts at remarkable levels of coherence and quality.

It is important that the ChatGPT model's algorithms are continuously refined and improved to ensure that they are ethical and do not have biases. This will allow it to be a valuable and responsible tool for society.

Machine learning is a subdiscipline within AI. It is a process utilized to improve algorithms by analyzing and learning from large sets of data. This technology is built on advanced models that make predictions and utilize minimal human intervention. The machines are able to learn through transformations and provide the desired outputs.

Machine learning can be used in various ways in today's society. For example, Google searches use machine learning for its autocomplete and predictive capabilities.

Autocomplete is a feature that allows users to type the first couple of letters of their query to get the results they are looking for. Google was the first company to implement this feature. Now, almost every search engine has it. Other companies such as Amazon, Spotify, and Flipkart also have it.

In machine learning, Google's predictive search works seamlessly with autocomplete. It uses algorithms developed after analyzing user behavior to predict what they might do next. For instance, by studying the way people watch movies, Netflix can provide recommendations based on their analysis.

In machine learning, ChatGPT can be used to improve the performance of models by performing similar operations. This will make the process of predictive search and autocomplete easier.

ChatGPT and Machine Learning

Machine learning is being used to train ChatGPT, which is based on a massive amount of data. This dataset features various language models that can be utilized to generate human-like conversations.

The difference between supervised and unsupervised learning is that the former is more stable.

ChatGPT's developers combine the unsupervised and supervised learning to improve the chatbot's capabilities. Through this method, they can learn from the data and provide refined results.

ChatGPT utilizes supervised learning. Models are trained by labeling data, and these are then expected to predict future outcomes based on new inputs. The program uses reinforcement learning techniques known as RLHF in its training loop.

RLHF is a machine learning technique that enhances the AI language model's ability to converse. Developers of ChatGPT use this method by providing a feedback loop, which instructs the chatbot on how to distinguish between an incorrect response and a correct one.

The developers of ChatGPT utilize a reward model, wherein the AI is incentivized if it produces a correct answer and a positive one. Conversely, it is given a low reward if it produces a wrong response. By learning from the reward system, the chatbot can then provide refined outputs.

Through the use of RLHF, ChatGPT can now provide more human-like responses. This method works by modifying the output of the model in response to the input provided by human trainers. During the chatbot's initial training phase, human instructors take on the roles of AI assistants and users.

Weak AI and Strong AI

Artificial intelligence that is weak can perform simple tasks. This type of AI, also known as narrow AI or ANI, is made by algorithms that are made by humans. It can perform only predefined actions by simulating intelligence.

Compared to weak AI that is made using human-made algorithms, strong AI has the capability to develop mental capabilities. This is because it can mimic the thoughts and actions of a person's brain. Although it doesn't have natural consciousness, strong AI can still function properly by receiving and processing data. This means it can trigger a learning process by absorbing information.

One example is an advanced narrow ChatGPT, which can generate responses to text-based prompts. Its ability to process natural language makes it a particularly powerful AI. It can also understand and mimic the style and tone of the prompt.

For instance, ChatGPT can provide a helpful response to our query about our feeling "sad". Not only did it understand our message, but it also delivered an empathetic response. This is because it has been trained to respond to emotional prompts in a way that is both relatable and conversational.

When ChatGPT is asked to write an article about making people "cheerful", it uses a different tone. It knows that the query is no longer "you being sad" but "people being sad."

The ChatGPT system demonstrates the efficacy of an advanced narrow AI by utilizing a vast corpus of data to analyze human-like responses.

Through machine learning, ChatGPT can learn about the nuances of natural language processing (NLP). It can then use these algorithms to produce the desired output. Moreover, its learning abilities help it improve the quality of its output.

This section discussed the importance of machine learning in helping ChatGPT become a formidable type of AI. By utilizing this technology, ChatGPT can now identify patterns in data, which significantly improves its performance over time.

Some of the advantages of ChatGPT's machine learning capabilities are listed here:

- Through its machine learning capabilities, ChatGPT can provide personalized responses to inquiries made in the customer service and e-commerce sectors.

- Through its machine learning capabilities, ChatGPT can create effective online content and marketing campaigns. It can analyze trends and present relevant social media strategies.

- In today's digital age, educators need to use technology to enhance the quality of their teaching. With the help of machine learning, they can now identify the learning needs of their students and develop effective curriculums.

- In the healthcare industry, machine learning can be utilized to collect and analyze data. It can then be used by medical professionals to provide more effective and personalized advice.

- For machine learning, ChatGPT can be utilized for providing financial advice and studying market trends.

This article aims to discuss the relationship between machine learning and ChatGPT. The latter's ability to improve its responses is a vital part of its operation. With the help of ML, ChatGPT can enhance its customer experience, provide more accurate and personalized responses, and improve its search query capabilities.

ChatGPT in Natural Language Processing

ChatGPT is an advanced language model that is designed to process and generate human-type text responses. It was developed by OpenAI, and it utilizes a deep neural network framework known as the transformer architecture.

With ChatGPT, you can create coherent text, engage in conversations that are context-aware, and answer questions that are related to NLP. It is ideal for various tasks, such as translation and content generation, and it can be used in virtual assistants and chatbots.

ChatGPT is useful for researchers and companies that want to take advantage of the power of AI-driven generation and understanding in language. It exhibits the continuous evolution of NLP techniques, which will help us make meaningful and natural interactions between humans and computers.

Text-based conversations are commonly used with ChatGPT, which is designed to facilitate conversations. It can comprehend verbal cues and produce relevant responses in a manner suitable for virtual assistants, chatbots, and other such AI applications.

The ChatGPT framework uses a deep neural network known as the transformer architecture. It is capable of handling sequential data and is well-suited for generating and understanding human language.

ChatGPT has been trained on a vast amount of textual data extracted from the Internet, which covers a wide range of topics and languages. This knowledge helps it understand the human language's nuances, such as context and grammar.

The ChatGPT framework has a large number of parameters, which enables it to study intricate textual connections and patterns. Its exceptional language creation abilities can be attributed to its remarkable size.

While ChatGPT is designed to work on general datasets, it can also be customized to handle specific domains or tasks. This allows it to adapt to the needs of different industries, such as healthcare and finance.

ChatGPT excels at contextual understanding, which is important when developing coherent and contextualized responses in extended conversations. It can maintain the context of the dialogue over multiple turns.

ChatGPT utilizes methods for reinforcement learning, which lets it enhance its responses whenever users interact with it. It can also learn from feedback to improve its performance.

The ability to support different languages makes ChatGPT an ideal tool for global platforms. This enables it to comprehend and produce text in different languages, facilitating cultural exchange. ChatGPT is capable of producing text for different tasks, such as content creation.

Current Applications of ChatGPT for NLP Tasks

Sentiment analysis is a process utilized in business to identify the emotional tone behind a text message and categorize it into neutral, positive, or negative. It is a vital part of any organization's language processing efforts to understand how consumers perceive and interact with its offerings.

Because of the complexity of customer feedback, it is often difficult to identify which words are meant to be a backhanded compliment or a mild expression. With the help of large language models, they can easily address this issue. See Figure 2-1.

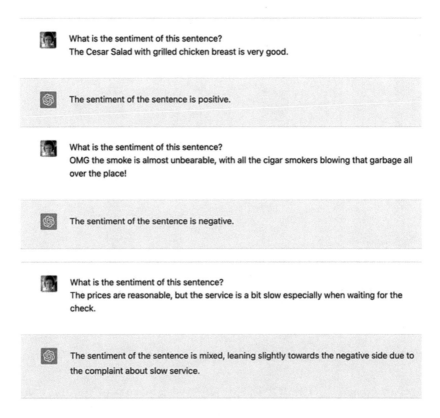

Figure 2-1. *ChatGPT in sentiment analysis*

An approach known as *aspect-based sentiment analysis* (ABSA) is utilized in NLP to classify the sentiments of a text. Unlike other methods, which analyze emotions, this method doesn't treat text as an entire entity. Instead, it can talk about the various aspects of a service or product.

Through the use of the ChatGPT and NLP models, a company can create a sentiment analysis pipeline that can analyze the various aspects of a product or service. It can then identify the features that its customers most likely dislike or prefer. See Figure 2-2.

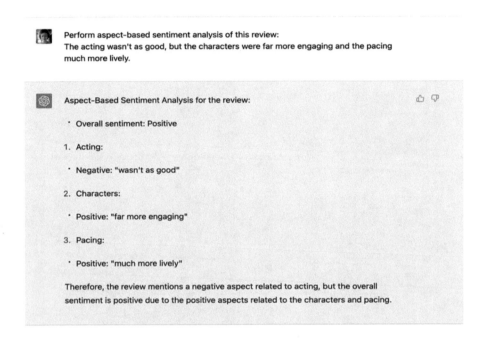

Figure 2-2. *ChatGPT using aspect-based analysis*

One of the uses of ChatGPT is for NER, which is a process that involves identifying and grouping words or phrases in a text analysis. This can be useful for identifying and organizing various organizations, people, locations, and more.

One of the most common applications of natural language processing is analyzing clinical data. Basal Metabolic Rate (BMR) is a challenging task because of how complex biomedical language is, as well as how many entities can appear in text.

Through extensive training on a large corpus, ChatGPT has been able to achieve high-quality NER labeling, which can help identify and categorize drugs and diseases. See Figure 2-3.

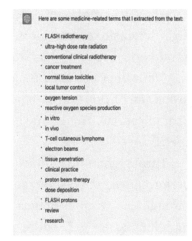

Figure 2-3.   *ChatGPT in NER*

ChatGPT in Neural Networks

The breakthrough achievement of ChatGPT demonstrates the exceptional capabilities of deep learning frameworks. It is based on the transformer framework, which revolutionized the field of NLP.

The transformer architecture was first presented in the seminal work of Vaswani and colleagues, "Attention Is All That You Need." This type of network architecture is ideal for handling sequential data.

The ChatGPT framework features a multilayered structure that includes components such as feedforward neural networks and self-attention systems. This allows it to perform contextual and hierarchical extractions from text.

The main focus of the transformer framework is on its attention mechanisms, which allow it to weigh the significance of each word and token in an input sequence. This enables the model to concentrate on the relevant context and produce coherent language.

ChatGPT's embedding layer converts input words into vectors with high-dimensional structures. By doing this, the words can be considered as numerical values, which makes them suitable for network processing.

While the ChatGPT framework is pre-trained on a vast corpus of text, it can be fine-tuned to perform specific tasks in specific domains or applications. This allows it to enhance its performance and tailor it to specific needs.

Through reinforcement learning, ChatGPT can improve its performance in user interactions. It is continuously updated and refined through real-world feedback. The ability to generate and understand multilingual text is a feature of ChatGPT. It demonstrates the flexibility of the transformer framework and its global appeal.

The extensive training data and neural network architecture of ChatGPT have allowed it to achieve high-level performance on various tasks and benchmarks. This has further cemented its place as a pioneering model in the field of natural language processing.

The deep rooted structure of the ChatGPT framework, which is based on the transformer concept, has revolutionized the way natural language processing is done. Its ability to process text and produce human-like content has wide-reaching applications, such as virtual assistants and chatbots. It sets new standards for what is possible in the field of AI-driven natural language generation and understanding.

Neural networks are often talked about as a vital component of AI. Fundamentally, it's a collection of nodes that lets a computer recognize patterns in data and learn from examples. The ChatGPT model, which is a transformer-based AI framework, is no different.

A neural network is an AI system that takes a cue from the nervous system and brain. It uses its interconnected functions to process data and produce desired outputs, which is similar to the brain's neurons. It has applications in various fields, such as medical diagnosis and speech recognition.

The ChatGPT model employs feedforward and normalization layers to deliver human-like responses. The latter enables the learning of complex patterns by applying a nonlinear transformation. Furthermore, the normalization layer ensures that the input values are uniform across all the training modules.

Before it can be used in public, ChatGPT undergoes a pre-training process to ensure it performs as expected. It handles text input through various steps, such as encoding, tokenization, output generation, and probability distribution.

The technologies that are related to machine learning and AI are closely tied to each other. The rise of neural networks has been attributed to the data landscape that has been created by the rise of high-performance computing and big data. These platforms have allowed developers to train complex networks by collecting and storing vast amounts of information.

The ChatGPT framework is based on the principles of machine learning and neural networks. It uses this approach to train its neural network to recognize and respond to text input. Fine-tuning the system's performance is also important to ensure that it can accurately perform on specific types of inputs.

ChatGPT's technology is built on the principles of machine learning and neural networks. Neural networks are artificial intelligence systems that are modeled after the functions and structures of the human brain. These are interconnected nodes that carry information.

ChatGPT uses a neural network to analyze and comprehend language. It learns by studying a vast amount of textual information, such as online conversations and news articles. The network then makes predictions about language and recognizes patterns.

Machine learning is a process that involves teaching a neural network how to recognize and respond to various types of language.

ChatGPT learns by analyzing the user's inputs and identifying the key points in the message. Upon its comprehension of the subject, it produces a response based on its knowledge base.

Autoregression is a process that ChatGPT uses to generate its responses. This method involves coming up with a single word at a time based on the preceding sentences. This ensures that its responses are grammatically correct and also resonate in the context of a conversation.

The ability to adapt and learn is one of the main advantages of ChatGPT's technology. It is constantly fed with new text data, which helps it improve its comprehension of language and produce more accurate and relevant answers.

Autoregression is a method that ChatGPT employs to generate its answers. It formulates responses by coming up with a single term at a time, with the aim of ensuring that its utterances resonate coherently and are grammatically correct.

ChatGPT's ability to produce responses that accurately and thoroughly mimic the written word is another advantage of its technology. This is accomplished through a process known as *natural language generation,* which involves the use of complex algorithms.

The ChatGPT system first generates a list of words and phrases that it can use in its response. It then uses various algorithms to rank the candidates according to their relevance and grammatical correctness.

After ranking the candidates, ChatGPT uses autoregression to select the best one to produce one response at a time. It aims to ensure that the answer meets both its contextual relevance and grammatically correct standards.

The ChatGPT system faces one of its main challenges when it comes to producing accurate and relevant answers for users. To address this issue, it employs different techniques to improve its output over time.

Fine-tuning is a process that's used to train the neural network to respond better to specific types of inputs. By doing this, ChatGPT can enhance its ability to provide more accurate and helpful answers to consumers.

Besides producing answers, ChatGPT can also be utilized for other natural language processing applications, such as translation and summarization. Developers can make virtual assistants and chatbots that can comprehend and respond to queries in a more natural manner with the help of this technology.

ChatGPT is an AI-based chatbot that can answer queries by analyzing and understanding natural language. Its model is based on a transformer, which is capable of processing entire sentences at the same time. ChatGPT can be utilized for a wide range of applications, such as virtual assistants and chatbots. Developers can make these kinds of applications work seamlessly by integrating ChatGPT.

Technology Architecture of ChatGPT

The ChatGPT framework is composed of various technologies and components. It enables a sophisticated AI system by integrating deep learning, which is subset of ML, and other related technologies.

The ChatGPT framework is powered by deep learning, a type of machine learning that utilizes neural networks with numerous layers to process and comprehend vast amounts of information. Deep learning is commonly used for language comprehension and modeling.

The ChatGPT architecture is built on the transformer model, a widely used framework for modeling and analyzing complex sentences. It has revolutionized the way natural language processing is performed. The model's self-attention mechanism helps it analyze and interpret the different words in sentences.

The ChatGPT framework goes through a two-step training process. The first phase involves learning the fundamentals of grammar, context, and language, and this is done before it can start working on specific tasks. During the fine-tuning phase, the model is trained on specific datasets to improve its performance in areas such as customer support, healthcare, and legal.

The different attention mechanisms are implemented in the transformer model's layers to capture the context and dependencies in the text. They can be used to understand complex connections between words.

The ChatGPT framework converts tokenized input into numerical vectors through the use of embedded layers. These layers are ideal for neural network analysis due to their semantic link preservation.

The ChatGPT framework employs reinforcement learning methods to enhance the model's responses when interacting with users. It then gets feedback on its performance, and it uses this to improve its contextual responses.

Developers can easily integrate the ChatGPT framework into their applications using an API. This allows them to extend the model's capabilities into their services and products.

The framework's design features various safety and ethical considerations to minimize the effects of harmful content generation and biases. OpenAI has put in place safeguards to ensure that the technology is used ethically.

The ChatGPT framework is designed to work seamlessly with various languages. This allows it to meet the diverse linguistic needs of its users.

The ChatGPT technology architecture is composed of deep learning, reinforcement learning, attention mechanisms, and various ethical considerations. This ensures that the framework can perform remarkably well in natural language processing tasks.

Architecture of ChatGPT in Neural Networks

As mentioned, the ChatGPT architecture is based on the transformer framework, which has revolutionized the field of natural language processing. This overview talks about the architecture's significance within the realm of neural networks.

The neural network's input layer is composed of a section that accepts text-based instructions from users. These instructions can be queries or messages.

The text input is tokenized, which breaks it down into smaller parts like subwords or words. This allows the model to perform structured text processing.

The transformation of the encoded text into a format suitable for neural networks is carried out by an embedding layer. It converts the encoded text into a vector that can be understood and processed by the neural networks.

The ChatGPT architecture's core structure features numerous transformer-like elements.

The model's response generation process involves implementing decoding techniques on the output tokens. These methods are usually carried out by using algorithms such as beam search or greedy decoding. After the selected tokens are extracted, the model's response is written in a human-readable form.

Through reinforcement learning and fine-tuning, ChatGPT can improve its performance on specific tasks and domains. This process can also be used to improve the model's responses in response to user interactions.

The transformer framework is the core structure of ChatGPT, which is used for its generation and comprehension capabilities in natural language. It is an ideal choice for developing applications that are focused on providing a variety of NLP services, such as virtual assistants and chatbots.

Summary

With this, we have come to the end of this chapter. You have gained a historical understanding of the ChatGPT technology including machine learning algorithms, natural language processing, and neural networks. In the upcoming chapter, you will learn about the applications of ChatGPT in software development, customer support, creative writing, HR operations, and other industries.

CHAPTER 3

Real-World Applications for ChatGPT

After taking a deep dive into technological aspects of ChatGPT, this new chapter focuses on the real-world applications of ChatGPT. It makes sense to apply technology in real-life use cases to see its advantages. In this chapter, we will identify some use cases in the fields of software development, customer support, content creation, HR operations, travel and tourism, and others to see how ChatGPT benefits users and creates great user experience. AI is a promising technology that can assist in various tasks and can automate many other activities. One of the most popular generative AI models is ChatGPT, which was released in November 2022.

In this chapter, we will talk about the 10 most common uses of ChatGPT in various industries. If you are planning on using your company's data for the development of generative AI, then you can investigate investing in training and optimizing large language models.

© Charles Waghmare 2023
C. Waghmare, *Unleashing The Power of ChatGPT*,
https://doi.org/10.1007/979-8-8688-0032-0_3

Software Development

In software development, utilizing ChatGPT involves integrating it into your workflow or application to carry out specific tasks related to natural language processing. We will talk about how to utilize this feature in more ways than one.

- You can use an API from OpenAI or a library from the Python platform. The latter allows you to interact with the ChatGPT model directly by writing code.

- To use the OpenAI API, you must first sign up. You will then be asked to provide an API key, which will be used to verify your requests.

- The API request will be made using the specified library or endpoint. It should contain the necessary input text and instructions that you want to provide to the ChatGPT model.

- After you've made the API request, the ChatGPT response will be sent to you. This will allow you to collect and process the data that was generated by the program.

- To minimize the impact of errors and limit the number of requests sent to the API, you should implement effective error handling and rate-limiting methods in your code.

- You can integrate the ChatGPT feature into your application or development process. You can use it to create code snippets, provide user interfaces, automate content creation, and offer support.

- Follow a comprehensive testing process to ensure that
  the integration works properly. You can also adjust
  the parameters and instructions depending on the
  requirements and the user experience.

- Prior to integrating the ChatGPT framework into your
  application or workflow, ensure that you abide by
  the terms and conditions of the OpenAI or other AI
  language model provider.

In case you're planning on using ChatGPT in your application
development, make sure you consider its various biases and limitations.
You must also ensure that the security and privacy of the collected data are
protected.

Figure 3-1 shows you how to integrate ChatGPT's capabilities into your
existing software projects.

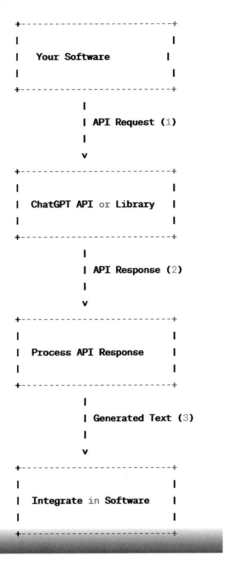

Figure 3-1. *Flowchart explaining usage of ChatGPT in software development*

As explained in Figure 3-1, these are the steps:

1. The API request made by your software application to ChatGPT is composed of the prompt and the specific settings or instructions that you want to provide to the language model.

2. The response is generated by ChatGPT after the request has been processed. It contains the output generated by the model according to the provided input.

3. The API response is then processed by your application to retrieve the output or information that was generated by ChatGPT.

4. The output from ChatGPT may include translating, code generation, text completion, or other language-related tasks, and it can be utilized in your application.

5. The output of ChatGPT may be integrated into your application as required. This can be done by displaying it in a manner that's natural to the user, or it can be utilized as part of an automated content creation process.

Customer Support

Integrating ChatGPT into a customer support department can result in enhanced interactions with clients and better services.

6. Before you start using ChatGPT in a customer support department, identify the various use cases that it can help with. For instance, it can be used to provide helpful answers to frequently asked questions or guide users through troubleshooting.

7. Before you implement ChatGPT in a support department, make sure the model is thoroughly tuned to your historical data. Doing so will allow it to understand the context and language of your company's support operations.

8. Create a user interface for ChatGPT that will allow agents to interact with it. This can be done through an interface that will be integrated into existing software or a separate dashboard.

9. ChatGPT can automate the routine handling of customer inquiries by providing predefined answers to commonly asked questions. This can help free up human support staff members to focus on more complicated issues and improve customer service.

10. An escalation mechanism will allow agents to take on more sensitive or challenging inquiries from ChatGPT and handle such issues in a more appropriate manner. This will ensure that your customers get the personalized attention they need.

11. One of the most important steps that you should take when it comes to implementing ChatGPT in your support department is to have trained agents review and supervise the responses generated by the system. This will help ensure that the responses are correct and error-free.

12. Follow a continuous improvement strategy by regularly gathering feedback from your customers and support agents about the performance of ChatGPT. This will help you improve the model and meet the needs of your customers.

13. Providing information about the use of ChatGPT during support inquiries can help customers feel valued and encouraged to speak with the chatbot. Transparency can also set the right tone and reduce frustration in the event that clients prefer to speak with a human agent.

14. When handling sensitive data, ensure that ChatGPT has been trained and configured to do so in a secure manner. If necessary, anonymization can be implemented.

15. Follow a regular maintenance strategy to keep your ChatGPT up-to-date with the latest support data. This will allow you to continuously improve the model and meet the needs of your customers.

Integrating ChatGPT into your customer support function can result in better services and efficiency. But it's important to strike a balance between the need to automate and human support to guarantee a favorable experience for customers. Figure 3-2 illustrates the steps to use ChatGPT in a customer support department.

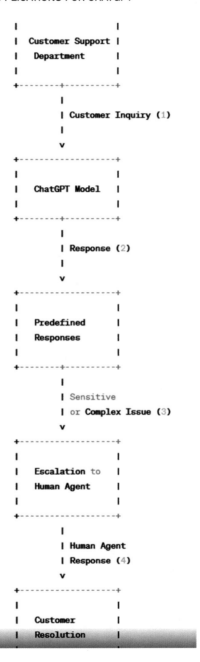

Figure 3-2. *Flowchart of how customer support can adopt ChatGPT*

The figure indicates the following:

1. Users can initiate a support query through email, chat, or other forms of communication using ChatGPT.

2. The ChatGPT model takes the customer's query and generates a response using its language capabilities.

3. ChatGPT offers predefined responses for straightforward and common inquiries, which helps the system automatically handle such questions.

4. If the chat request is sensitive or if the customer has a complex issue, the ChatGPT system can automatically escalate the query to a human support agent.

5. The escalated query is then forwarded to a human agent within the customer support group, who will handle the conversation.

6. The customer support agent responds to the query with a personalized answer that addresses the customer's complex problem.

7. The support process will continue until the customer's issue is resolved.

This method will help you handle routine inquiries while also offering the option to humanize the response to sensitive or complex issues. In addition to reducing the support agent workload, this approach will enhance the customer experience and boost response time.

HR Operations

With the help of ChatGPT, HR operations can optimize their processes and enhance their efficiency. There are several ways to implement this feature in your organization.

1. ChatGPT can be used to connect with job applicants and collect information about their availability, experience, and qualifications. This will help in identifying the ideal candidates for certain positions.

2. Integrating ChatGPT into your job portal or career website can provide candidates with in-depth explanations of the application process, benefits, and company culture.

3. Implementing an employee onboarding assistant that is powered by ChatGPT can help new hires navigate the process and provide them with the necessary information and answers to their queries.

4. Implementing a ChatGPT-powered employee development assistant would help promote the acquisition of new knowledge and skills by providing relevant resources and training materials.

5. ChatGPT can be utilized to provide staff members with details about company policies, including benefits and leave policies.

6. Implementing ChatGPT in performance management will help remind workers about upcoming reviews, deadlines, and strategies to enhance their performance.

7. Collect employee feedback through surveys and use ChatGPT to get insights into their engagement and satisfaction.

8. Create an HR help desk powered by ChatGPT to provide staff members with assistance with common queries, such as accessing payroll records and requesting leave.

9. Exit interviews and onboarding can be facilitated by ChatGPT. This will help employees explore the offboarding process while also collecting valuable feedback.

10. ChatGPT can be utilized by integrating with performance management systems to recognize achievements, remind workers about company events, and provide them with recognition information and rewards.

11. In case your company has an international workforce, you may utilize ChatGPT to communicate with staff members who don't speak English.

12. ChatGPT may be utilized to generate reports related to employee performance, leave summaries, and workforce analytics.

While ChatGPT may be helpful in various HR tasks, it must complement the efforts of human staff members to be successful. In addition, it should be noted that ChatGPT should not replace the involvement and supervision of human staff members in handling sensitive matters.

Travel and Tourism

The ChatGPT platform can be utilized in the tourism industry to enhance the experience of travelers and other stakeholders.

1. As a virtual guide, ChatGPT can help travelers find local events, activities, and attractions based on their preferences.

2. ChatGPT can help individuals plan their trips by suggesting ideal itineraries, facilitating transfers, and providing insights into the ideal travel dates across various locations.

3. ChatGPT may be utilized to assist travelers in conversing with locals and navigating language barriers.

4. Travelers can utilize ChatGPT to research a destination and gain knowledge about its history, customs, and safety guidelines.

5. ChatGPT can also provide users with real-time weather reports, allowing them to plan their trip according to the conditions.

6. Notifications and travel alerts can be sent by ChatGPT. These can notify users about gate changes, flight delays, and other pertinent updates.

7. Accommodation and hotel recommendations can be requested by users depending on their budgets.

8. Users can be notified about local festivals and events, as well as cultural celebrations that are happening at their chosen destination.

9. ChatGPT can suggest local establishments and dishes that cater to specific dietary requirements.

10. ChatGPT can offer helpful travel advice, such as emergency numbers and travel insurance details, to help passengers navigate the world safely.

11. Users can obtain travel testimonials and reviews from other people to help make informed decisions when traveling.

12. ChatGPT can endorse sustainable practices, encouraging individuals to make responsible decisions while traveling and promoting eco-friendly choices.

13. ChatGPT can also provide immersive experiences and virtual tours for travelers who cannot physically visit certain locations.

14. Tourism organizations and agencies can utilize ChatGPT to provide assistance and answer questions in an efficient manner.

Through the integration of ChatGPT technology into the tourism sector (see Figure 3-3), businesses can offer travelers individualized and timely assistance, increase their customer satisfaction, and improve the overall travel experience.

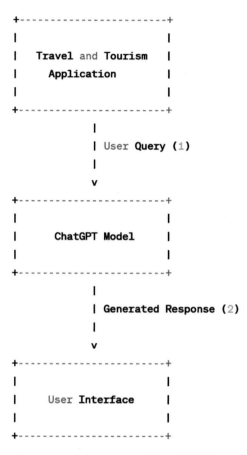

Figure 3-3. *Flowchart on how to use ChatGPT for travel and tourism*

The figure indicates the following:

1. When a traveler interacts with the tourism application, they are prompted to provide a query to get more information or guidance related to their trip.

2. The user's query is then sent to the ChatGPT framework, which takes into account the input and produces a response that's based on its comprehension of the language.

3. The ChatGPT framework then produces a response that consists of recommendations, travel itineraries, and other pertinent details based on the traveler's query.

4. The generated response is then presented to the traveler using the tourism application's user interface, which can be accessed through various platforms such as a web page, chat window, or mobile app.

Travelers can converse with ChatGPT to receive personalized recommendations, itineraries, language translation, safety tips, local events updates, and other helpful details to make their trips more enjoyable. It acts as a virtual assistant that offers valuable insight and assistance to make one's trip more informed and enjoyable.

Operations

ChatGPT can help organizations improve their efficiency and streamline various processes. There are several ways to utilize this technology in operations.

1. Implementing ChatGPT will automate the process of handling routine customer support inquiries, allowing human employees to focus on more critical issues.

2. Use ChatGPT to automate various repetitive tasks, such as email responses and data entry. It can help boost productivity and reduce the amount of time spent on manual work.

3. ChatGPT can be utilized to facilitate proficient language translation to engage with stakeholders, global partners, and customers.

4. To provide employees with a deeper understanding of the ChatGPT platform, create a knowledge base that includes FAQs.

5. New employees should be trained using a chatbot-powered onboarding assistant. This will help them navigate the initial steps of their employment and provide them with essential resources.

6. ChatGPT can be used to organize meetings and set reminders, making it easier for people to schedule appointments and tasks.

7. ChatGPT can also be utilized to analyze and generate insights, helping organizations formulate business plans and make decisions.

8. By integrating ChatGPT into the project management system, team members can be kept up with the status of the project and its various tasks and deadlines. Integration requires development.

9. Organizations can optimize their supply chain operations by using ChatGPT to monitor inventory and manage orders.

10. Organizations can ensure compliance with regulations and standards by carrying out inspections and quality control checks.

11. HR departments can leverage ChatGPT to carry out various HR-related activities, such as employee feedback collection, recruitment screening, and policy inquiries.

12. Implementing ChatGPT will help provide staff members with troubleshooting assistance and IT support.

13. You can carry out regulatory compliance checks and risk assessments.

14. ChatGPT can be utilized to manage the procurement process and communicate with vendors.

15. ChatGPT can be deployed to generate reports and monitor KPIs.

Before implementing ChatGPT in an operational environment, it's important to ensure that the security and privacy of your data is protected. Also, regular performance appraisals should be carried out. Through the integration of ChatGPT into certain processes, companies can enhance their customer experiences, boost their productivity, and optimize their business operations.

Figure 3-4 depicts how to adopt ChatGPT for operations management.

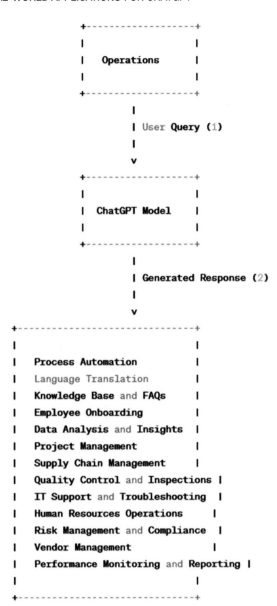

Figure 3-4. *Flowchart for ChatGPT operations management*

A user query is a type of interaction that allows an employee or customer to ask for assistance.

1. The user query is sent to the ChatGPT framework, which takes into account the input and produces a response based on its comprehension of the language.

2. The ChatGPT framework generates a response that is geared toward providing the requested information or instructions.

3. Integrating ChatGPT into an operational process can result in streamlined tasks and decreased manual intervention.

4. ChatGPT can help with language translation, which can facilitate better communication with stakeholders and international partners.

5. ChatGPT can also help with FAQs and a knowledge base, which will allow employees to quickly find answers to frequently asked questions.

6. As an onboarding assistant, ChatGPT can help new employees navigate the process and provide them with necessary training materials.

7. ChatGPT is also capable of analyzing and providing insight into data to help improve business decisions.

8. Integrating ChatGPT into a project management application can allow team members to keep track of the status of the project.

9. ChatGPT may be utilized for the management of supply chain functions, such as order optimization and inventory tracking.

10. ChatGPT may be utilized to carry out inspections and quality control checks to ensure adherence to certain standards.

11. ChatGPT can also provide staff with troubleshooting assistance and IT support.

12. Human resources functions can be handled by ChatGPT. This includes conducting interviews, collecting feedback from employees, and conducting policy inquiries.

13. ChatGPT can help with regulatory compliance and risk assessment.

14. ChatGPT may handle the management of procurement processes, including communicating with vendors.

15. ChatGPT may analyze key KPIs and produce reports.

Improving an organization's processes and offering better support to consumers can be achieved through the integration of ChatGPT into an operational environment. Nevertheless, it is crucial to ensure the security of data, keep human oversight in mind, and carefully evaluate the effectiveness and efficiency of ChatGPT in certain circumstances.

Marketing

ChatGPT can be utilized for marketing to provide customized experiences, optimize campaigns, and engage consumers. There are many ways to take advantage of this platform.

1. ChatGPT is a chatbot platform that enables organizations to engage their customers in real time through conversations and provide them with product information.

2. ChatGPT can also be used to create content for various marketing materials, including blog posts, newsletters, and social media updates.

3. By utilizing ChatGPT and artificial intelligence, a company can conceptualize a customized recommendation system that takes into account the customer's past behavior and preferences to suggest goods or services.

4. Use ChatGPT to generate leads by delivering surveys, interactive quizzes, or other forms that can engage participants.

5. Conduct surveys and collect feedback through ChatGPT to enhance services or goods based on the insights gained from customers.

6. ChatGPT can be integrated into an organization's social media management platform to handle FAQs, respond to messages, and interact with followers.

7. Using ChatGPT for email marketing, you can create dynamic and personalized content tailored to each client's preferences.

8. ChatGPT can be utilized to generate and test variations in advertisement copy to improve its effectiveness in online marketing campaigns.

9. ChatGPT can be used to generate brainstorming sessions and come up with testing concepts for marketing campaigns, landing pages, and product features.

10. ChatGPT can analyze customer sentiment and market trends through the processing of vast amounts of textual data.

11. Companies can segment their customers through ChatGPT, leveraging the platform's capabilities to analyze and target audiences based on their interests, behaviors, and preferences.

12. You can create virtual ambassadors or influencers using ChatGPT, who can represent your brand and interact with consumers.

13. Conduct contests and promotions in chat to build excitement around your brand and encourage customers to participate.

14. Cross-selling and upselling can be achieved through ChatGPT, as it lets you identify opportunities to sell to consumers based on their previous purchases.

15. By monitoring social media conversations and trends through ChatGPT, businesses can keep track of their customers' preferences and interests.

Make sure to maintain transparency while using ChatGPT for marketing (as in Figure 3-5), as customers should be aware of how the system works. You should also regularly assess the effectiveness of such strategies to see how they perform.

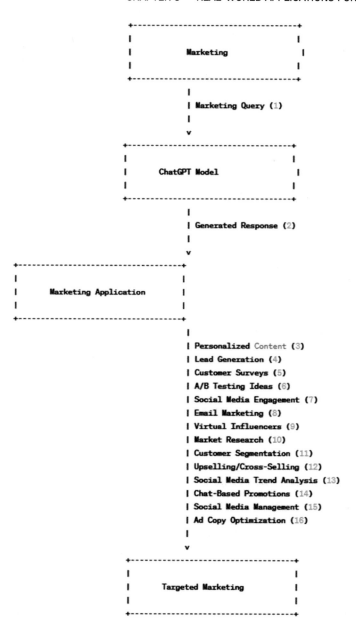

Figure 3-5. *Use of ChatGPT for marketing activities*

As per Figure 3-5, a marketing query is a request or request that a company makes to improve its ad copy or create content. This step usually involves conducting surveys or engaging with customers.

1. The ChatGPT model takes the marketing query and processes the input. It then generates relevant responses based on its comprehension of the language.

2. ChatGPT can then generate responses that offer solutions or information to marketing inquiries.

3. The generated responses are then incorporated into a marketing application, which performs various tasks and strategies.

4. ChatGPT can be utilized to create individualized content for social media, newsletters, blogs, and other promotional materials.

5. The ChatGPT platform can be utilized to engage consumers through surveys, interactive quizzes, or forms, ultimately leading to leads.

6. ChatGPT can be utilized to conduct surveys and collect feedback from customers to help enhance marketing efforts.

7. ChatGPT may be utilized to create dynamic email content and assist in personalizing campaigns.

8. ChatGPT can also be utilized to create virtual ambassadors or virtual influencers who can interact with consumers.

9. Customer sentiment and market trends can be analyzed using ChatGPT. This provides insights for marketing campaigns.

10. By segmenting consumers through ChatGPT, companies can target their efforts precisely based on their preferences and behaviors.

11. Cross-selling and upselling can be identified using ChatGPT. It can ascertain prospects for these activities based on their interests.

12. Social media conversations and trends can be monitored through ChatGPT. Companies can then learn more about their customers' interests.

13. By implementing chat-based contests and promotions, a company can build buzz around its brand and encourage customers to participate.

14. Social media management can be achieved by utilizing ChatGPT to handle FAQs, messages, and comments, all of which foster active customer engagement.

15. ChatGPT can be utilized to test and improve ad copy variations, allowing companies to optimize their marketing efforts.

Integrating ChatGPT into a company's marketing efforts can result in increased customer interaction, customized approaches to content creation, and better data-driven decisions.

Sales

ChatGPT can help sales professionals improve their customer interactions and streamline their operations. There are a variety of ways to utilize this tool in sales management.

1. ChatGPT can help sales professionals qualify leads by collecting necessary information before they are sent to sales representatives.

2. ChatGPT can also help sales professionals nurture leads by delivering customized content and follow-up messages.

3. Build a sales assistant that is powered by ChatGPT that can answer FAQs and provide helpful product information.

4. ChatGPT can be used by sales professionals to engage with customers in a personalized manner, offering recommendations that are based on their preferences.

5. ChatGPT can be utilized by sales professionals to analyze historical data and market trends, which can help them make better decisions and improve their sales forecasting.

6. Identifying cross-selling and upselling opportunities can be achieved through ChatGPT. This tool can be used to analyze the buying habits and purchase history of consumers.

7. ChatGPT competitor analysis lets sales teams evaluate pricing, strategies, and competitor activities to make better decisions.

8. Sales performance analysis is a process that can be used to identify areas of improvement and enhance the efficiency of sales teams.

9. ChatGPT can be utilized to collect feedback after sales activities, which can help enhance the satisfaction of consumers and the sales process.

10. Build a virtual assistant that is powered by ChatGPT that can help sales representatives navigate through the sales process and provide helpful tips.

11. Incorporate ChatGPT to provide sales reps with resources and training materials, ensuring continual improvement.

12. ChatGPT can be integrated into a quote generation system, which enables sales personnel to quickly generate accurate quotes.

13. Sales meeting scheduling can be streamlined with the help of ChatGPT, which allows users to set appointments and schedule demos and follow-ups.

14. Identifying opportunities and bottlenecks in the sales funnel may be achieved with the help of ChatGPT.

15. ChatGPT can be utilized to generate reports and provide insights that can be used to refine a sales strategy.

When ChatGPT is used for sales management (see Figure 3-6), the balance between human interaction and automation has to be right. Sales professionals still need to be involved in building relationships and handling complicated transactions. To ensure that ChatGPT is meeting the needs of the company, it should be regularly evaluated and improved.

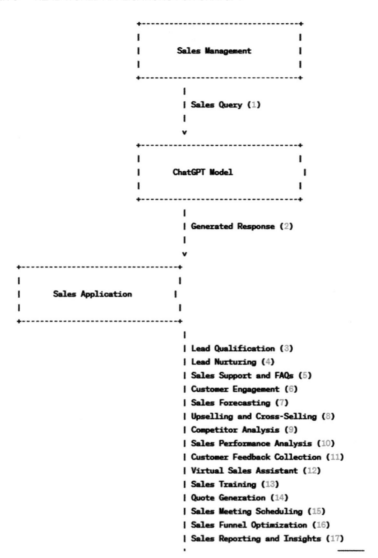

Figure 3-6. *ChatGPT for sales management*

As per Figure 3-6, a sales query is a process that starts with a potential customer's request for information. It can also include a lead inquiry and a sales-related question.

1. The ChatGPT model takes the sales query and processes the input. It then generates a response that's based on its comprehension of the language.

2. The ChatGPT model generates a response to provide sales-related questions with practical solutions or data.

3. The generated response is then incorporated into a sales application, which executes various sales strategies and tasks.

4. The ChatGPT model can be utilized to connect with and gather information with prospects for lead qualification.

5. The ChatGPT platform can nurture leads by delivering customized content and messages, keeping them engaged throughout the sales process.

6. ChatGPT can also help customers by providing product information and answers to frequently asked questions.

7. ChatGPT can be utilized to engage with consumers in real time, offering personalized recommendations and assistance.

8. You can analyze past market trends and sales data, presenting you with updated information to improve your sales predictions.

9. Through ChatGPT, a company can identify potential cross-selling and upselling opportunities with its existing customers.

10. Collect customer feedback through ChatGPT to enhance the efficiency of the sales process and boost the pleasure of consumers.

11. You can create a virtual sales assistant that's powered by ChatGPT to help sales personnel during sales calls.

12. You can also utilize ChatGPT to provide training materials to sales personnel.

13. You can integrate ChatGPT into a quote generation system, which will enable sales personnel to swiftly produce accurate quotes.

14. ChatGPT can be utilized to set up meetings, follow-ups, and demos, which can streamline the appointment-making process.

15. Sales funnel optimization involves leveraging ChatGPT to identify impediments and opportunities for enhanced efficiency.

16. You can also utilize ChatGPT to generate reports that can help with the refinement of your sales strategy.

Integrating ChatGPT into an organization's sales management system can help facilitate processes, increase customer interaction, and optimize sales tactics to achieve superior outcomes and boost consumer contentment. It is imperative to regularly assess ChatGPT's effectiveness and continuously enhance the system to accommodate specific business requirements and sales motifs.

Content Creation

A content creation process involves creating different types of written or digital content, such as blogs, vlogs, videos, infographics, and articles. The main objective of such work is to provide engaging, informative, and entertaining content that can appeal to specific audiences.

Before creating content, it's important to identify the target audience. This will help determine what kinds of content should be created. The content should have a clear objective. It should aim to entertain, educate, inform, generate leads, promote products, or raise brand awareness.

Before starting a content creation process, it's important to thoroughly research a chosen topic or subject. This step can help provide the necessary information to make the content more effective.

The creation phase is the time when the actual content is created. Depending on the medium, this can involve working on articles, videos, audio recordings, infographics, and more. Proofreading and editing are two of the most crucial steps in ensuring that the output is of high quality. They help identify spelling and grammatical mistakes and ensure coherence and accuracy.

Search engine optimization is a process that can help boost a website's visibility and attract more potential customers. The distribution and publishing of content can be done on various platforms, such as blogs, social media, and websites. Different strategies can also be utilized to reach a wider audience.

Social media promotion, email marketing, and collaborations are some of the methods that can be used to boost engagement and reach out to more people. Through analytical tools, such as web analytics, you can monitor the effectiveness of your content and gauge its impact and engagement, allowing you to make changes to improve it for the future.

Consistency in content production is important to maintain the engagement of your target audience and reach your goals. This involves research, creativity, and comprehension of the preferences and behaviors of your intended audience.

ChatGPT can be used for content creation. Figure 3-7 and Figure 3-8 show an example.

Figure 3-7. *Command prompt*

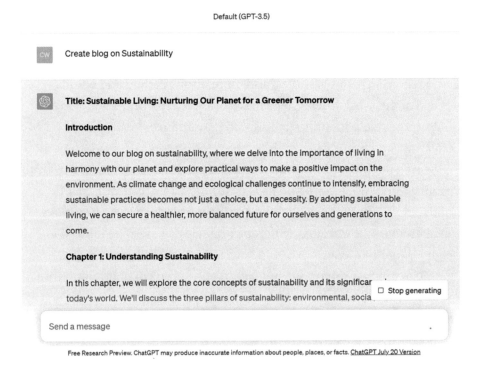

Figure 3-8. *Blog creation from ChatGPT*

Translation

Using ChatGPT for translation (see Figure 3-9) involves leveraging its generation capabilities. Although it's primarily focused on natural language understanding, it can still be utilized for translation between different languages.

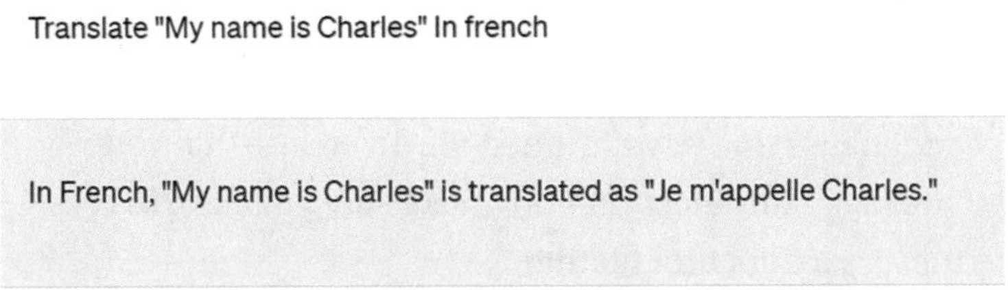

Translate "My name is Charles" In french

In French, "My name is Charles" is translated as "Je m'appelle Charles."

Figure 3-9. *Translation of English into French*

You can use ChatGPT for translation by following these steps:

1. Before you start working on a project, make sure you provide the text you want to translate. For instance, if you want to change the text in English to French, you must first specify which language the target is.

2. You can also interact with ChatGPT through a programming library or an API. OpenAI offers an API that can be used to generate language generation requests. After passing the source text, you must then translate the instructions into the desired language.

3. After receiving the ChatGPT response, the translated text will be put up for post-processing. This process can be performed depending on the requirements of the project.

4. Although ChatGPT can perform basic translations, it should be noted that it may not be as comprehensive or accurate as machine translation systems, such as Google Translate. For more advanced translations, it's advisable to use specialized models.

5. As of September 2021, ChatGPT performed language translation only on the supported languages that it was trained on. To ensure that you are using the latest version, make sure you have the necessary documentation.

Summary

In this chapter, you saw real-life applications of ChatGPT in the fields of software development, HR operations, travel and tourism, sales, marketing, operations, creative writing, and translation. Each real-life use case discussed how ChatGPT has improved the efficiency of businesses and how it has improved the user experience for end users.

CHAPTER 4

Enhancing Business Communication with ChatGPT

After exploring the practical aspects of ChatGPT in real-world scenarios such as in software development, customer support, creative writing, and other fields, in this chapter we will focus on how ChatGPT facilitates businesses to interact with their customers in a more natural and effective manner.

ChatGPT and AI: Unlocking Efficiency and Productivity

Today, businesses are constantly adapting to a fast-paced and response-oriented environment. Effective communication is therefore a vital component of any organization's strategy to ensure that it can compete effectively with its competitors. In an era where technological advancements are constantly taking place, improved tools and resources are being made available to help improve communication.

© Charles Waghmare 2023
C. Waghmare, *Unleashing The Power of ChatGPT*,
https://doi.org/10.1007/979-8-8688-0032-0_4

Artificial intelligence (AI) and ChatGPT are two examples of how technological advancements can help improve the way people communicate. These tools can allow individuals and companies to interact with each other in a completely different way. This section covers the various aspects of how AI and ChatGPT can help improve the way businesses communicate, including in the areas of customer support, internal communications, and data analysis.

Customer Support

One of the most critical aspects of any company is having a good customer support team. Unfortunately, many businesses struggle with maintaining effective support services because of a high volume of inquiries and inaccessibility. This can be challenging for the customers who need help the most.

Because of the increasing number of inquiries and the complexity of the support process, many companies such as Spotify, Mastercard, and Lyft are now using AI-powered chatbots to improve their customer service. These interactive platforms are able to answer a wide range of questions and provide helpful advice in just a few seconds.

With the use of these interactive platforms, customers no longer have to wait for a human to answer their questions. Instead, they can ask the chatbot directly about their concerns.

Marketing Emails

Effective marketing communication is vital in today's fast-paced world. AI has become a game-changer, and one of its most revolutionary applications is ChatGPT, which can improve the way companies promote themselves.

ChatGPT gives you the ability to create effective marketing emails with real-time suggestions and a streamlined writing process. The tool can help business communicators elevate their writing skills.

One of the biggest challenges that professionals face when it comes to creating effective emails is finding the right content. With the help of ChatGPT, they can easily create engaging content that will catch the attention of their potential clients.

With ChatGPT, they can easily fix grammar mistakes, refine language, and fine-tune the tone of their emails. This ensures that their communication is professional and aligns with their brand's image.

One of the most important factors that businesses consider when it comes to building strong connections is ensuring that their communications are consistent. With the help of ChatGPT, they can easily suggest consistent language and ensure that their emails are in line with their overall communication strategy.

Before using ChatGPT's services to write an email of any kind, make sure that you have clearly defined your objectives. This will ensure that the generated content will meet your goals.

Providing context to ChatGPT will result in more accurate and relevant suggestions. Explain your email's background, purpose, and tone to help the AI perceive your needs.

While ChatGPT provides a streamlined process for writing emails, it's still important to review and adjust the AI-generated work. Doing so will ensure that the final message aligns with the brand's message.

Dealing with Global Suppliers

Business crosses many borders in today's globalized world. With the help of ChatGPT's translation capabilities, businesses can reach out to their partners, stakeholders, and clients in different languages. These types of translations can help promote international collaboration and bridge language gaps.

Internal Communication

One of the most important factors that any company should consider when it comes to improving its internal communication is having effective collaboration. With the help of ChatGPT, employees can easily schedule meetings and send reminders with just a few clicks.

Automating some direct communication within the company will allow employees to focus on important tasks and meetings, which will result in better sales and service.

Data Analysis and Insights

ChatGPT is an AI-powered service that can analyze and interpret vast amounts of numerical and textual data. It can then draw useful conclusions from the information that it collects. Such systems can also identify trends and patterns in the exchanges between users on social media and in regular conversations.

Through ChatGPT, businesses can make informed decisions and enhance the quality of their products and services by collecting and analyzing customer feedback. E-commerce firms can take advantage of this platform by analyzing customer reviews to identify what their customers want and how they can adapt their product models to meet the changing market.

The goal of ChatGPT is to help businesses improve their customer satisfaction. It allows them to obtain the precise data they need to stay ahead of their competitors and keep up with the changes in the market.

The integration of AI and ChatGPT into business communication can help improve the way people interact with companies. AI can help organizations improve their internal processes, including the provision of multilingual assistance, data analysis, and customer support.

By integrating ChatGPT and AI into their operations, businesses can improve their processes and deliver the best possible services to their customers. They can also maintain a positive relationship with their employees. As AI and other technological advancements continue to develop, businesses should be ready to take advantage of these tools to create new opportunities.

Automating Communication with ChatGPT

In today's competitive environment, effective communication is vital. Whether it's with clients, with employees, or even within groups, being able to convey information quickly and efficiently is crucial to achieving success. But, what if we could automate some of the communication that businesses require, freeing up valuable resources for other tasks?"

With the emergence of ChatGPT, a revolutionary language model, companies are poised to redefine how they communicate.

This section aims to introduce ChatGPT, its capabilities, and what it can do with communication.

OpenAI developed ChatGPT, which is a massive language model that uses AI and machine learning to create and understand human-like content. It can be utilized to automate various tasks, such as responding to emails and answering customer support inquiries.

ChatGPT's ability to comprehend natural language is significant as it enables it to converse with others in a manner similar to how humans would do. This makes it an ideal tool for organizations looking to improve their communication efforts.

One of ChatGPT's most notable capabilities is its ability to create text. This is particularly useful as it can be utilized to produce blog posts, emails, and chatbot responses. It can be a tremendous resource saver as it can automate the tedious process of writing content.

Automating Customer Service Using ChatGPT

In customer service, ChatGPT is often utilized to train chatbots, which are computer programs that simulate human conversations. They can be integrated into an organization's app or website and can answer questions and resolve common issues.

One of the most common uses of ChatGPT in customer support is email automation. It can be used to respond to and understand emails sent by customers, which helps businesses handle a higher volume of inquiries.

In addition, ChatGPT can be utilized to generate scripts that can be used by customer service agents to provide accurate and consistent answers to frequently asked questions. This approach can result in a more pleasant experience for consumers and increase their satisfaction.

This section explores ChatGPT's various applications in enhancing customer support interactions, including email correspondence, chatbots, and script generation. In addition, it highlights the potential advantages, encompassing enhanced efficiency, improved client satisfaction, and 24-hour availability.

Automating Internal Communication

The section discusses the advantages of utilizing ChatGPT to automate internal communication within organizations.

One of the most important advantages of ChatGPT is its ability to improve the efficiency of internal communication. It can be used to automate various tasks, such as scheduling meetings and sending reminder messages. This can help employees focus on more important matters.

One of the most important benefits of ChatGPT is the ability to improve the consistency of internal communication. It's able to analyze and respond to the language used in the messages sent by an organization. This ensures that all communications are consistent with the company's brand and messaging.

Automated communication can result in fewer human errors. Also, ChatGPT can be utilized to send out important reminders and updates, which can help minimize the chances that vital information gets overlooked or missed.

Before you start implementing ChatGPT, it's important that you identify the various tasks and processes that will be automated. This can include the creation of content, internal communications, and customer service. After that, the ChatGPT model will be trained on how to understand the tone and language used by the organization.

After you've integrated ChatGPT into your existing processes, it's time to test the integration. This can involve integrating the chatbot into a company's app or website or integrating it into an email system that can automate responses. It's crucial to make any necessary changes and ensure the integration works seamlessly.

A maintenance and monitoring plan must be established for ChatGPT. This includes keeping track of its progress, identifying areas for growth, and continuously training the chatbot to improve its efficiency.

Notify the stakeholders and workers of the change and how it will affect them.

Technology Developments in ChatGPT

In the future, ChatGPT may be able to process natural language more effectively than today. This would allow it to respond to different kinds of expressions and provide more versatile services to companies.

One potential advancement is integrating computer vision technology into ChatGPT, which would enable it to comprehend and respond to texts and visual information. This will result in new opportunities for the automated recognition of objects and images.

In the future, there may be a capability for ChatGPT to be trained to respond in a more personalized manner, which would result in more human-like conversations.

Artificial intelligence and machine learning developments could also lead to the creation of more efficient and powerful language models, which would enhance ChatGPT's capabilities.

Advantages and Disadvantages of Automating Business Communication using ChatGPT

As companies strive to transform their operations and improve their customer experiences in the digital age, the rise of conversational AI has become a game-changing innovation.

The success of a company depends on effective communication. In the past, it was typically formal, lacked personal touch, and resulted in stilted and impersonal conversations. With the emergence of ChatGPT, business communication is no longer like this.

Advantages

With its ability to comprehend context, respond empathetically, and adjust to users' preferences, ChatGPT is a game-changing innovation. It can bridge the gap between stakeholders and businesses by conversing in a manner that feels human.

One of ChatGPT's main advantages is its ability to improve the productivity of various business functions. It can handle routine tasks and assist in internal operations, which can free up human resources for more complex work. By automating repetitive activities, ChatGPT helps companies reduce costs and improve their workflows.

Because of the fast pace of today's business environment, it is important that companies make fast and accurate decisions. With ChatGPT, they can do so by analyzing vast amounts of data in seconds, providing actionable recommendations and insights that can help them stay ahead of their competitors. It can also simulate scenarios and provide predictive analysis, which helps businesses identify potential opportunities and risks.

Strong relationships with stakeholders and customers are crucial for a company's success. With ChatGPT, businesses can elevate the experience of their customers by understanding their needs and providing recommendations tailored to suit them. Its multilingual capabilities can also help them interact with customers from different countries and overcome language barriers.

The rise of ChatGPT may also bring with it ethical issues such as related to privacy and personal data by collecting and processing data from website. To ensure that its development is conducted in a responsible manner, OpenAI has taken various steps to establish transparency and accountability. Organizations that use ChatGPT should prioritize the protection of their users' privacy, as well as other ethical guidelines like user consent and bias mitigation. When it comes to making effective use of ChatGPT, it is important that the company balances its efficiency with ethical considerations.

The emergence of ChatGPT signifies the beginning of a new era of business communication. It enables organizations to improve their efficiency, connect with their customers in a more meaningful manner, and develop new ideas. By adopting this technology, businesses can take advantage of the opportunities it presents.

Disadvantages

One company that uses ChatGPT is a customer support organization that has integrated it into their chatbot so that they can provide accurate and quick responses to their inquiries. This has helped them enhance their customer satisfaction.

A financial firm uses ChatGPT to organize meetings and send reminders as part of its internal communication strategy. It also handles other tasks such as taking minutes of meetings to improve the organization's consistency and efficiency.

The implementation cost of ChatGPT is another important aspect to consider. Although it can help organizations save time and resources, it can also come with a huge amount of training and integration fees.

Another aspect to consider is the possibility of errors or inaccuracies. Although ChatGPT can be a powerful tool, it can still be a machine learning model that doesn't always provide the correct responses. Having a system in place that can monitor and correct these errors is also important.

One of the biggest limitations of ChatGPT is its inability to respond to certain types of communication. This can be particularly problematic for companies that deal in a specific field.

Another issue that can be considered is the security of the data that an organization collects. Since ChatGPT requires a lot of data to train, it can be hard for companies to share this information with other companies.

It's important to keep in mind that ethical considerations must remain at the forefront. ChatGPT is poised to become an ally that can help businesses innovate and communicate in a new way.

How ChatGPT Is Transforming Business Communication

With ChatGPT, businesses can now improve how they interact with their employees, partners, and customers. It uses the power of AI and NLP to automate conversations, provide customized customer experiences, and answer inquiries in just a few seconds.

ChatGPT is a cost-effective and time-saving method that enables businesses to automate conversations. AI-powered chatbots can answer customer inquiries without requiring human intervention, leading to faster and more accurate responses to customers, ultimately improving the customer experience.

Businesses can enhance their customer service by utilizing ChatGPT. Through the use of AI-based methods, it can analyze data and produce customized responses that are likely to spark interest from clients, fostering relationships and promoting loyalty.

Businesses can lower their customer service expenses by implementing ChatGPT. It enables them to reduce the need for agents and associated costs by automating conversations, thus improving their bottom line.

In general, ChatGPT has revolutionized how companies interact with their workers, customers, and partners. By integrating the power of natural language processing and artificial intelligence, it enables organizations to automate conversations, generate personalized consumer experiences, and respond to inquiries from customers. Although it has some disadvantages, the positive aspects of ChatGPT outweigh its negative aspects.

Companies can now offer their customers personalized and automated services with ChatGPT, which can help improve their satisfaction and engagement.

Prior to utilizing ChatGPT, one must understand the fundamentals of AI-based communication. This encompasses comprehending the technology's capabilities, as well as how it can be utilized to engage consumers.

Before you start using ChatGPT, it's important that you thoroughly understand its basics. You should then create a chatbot that will allow customers to interact with it in a natural manner.

Companies can now leverage customer data to provide customized services, such as offering bargains and personalized recommendations.

Ensure that the chatbot is generating a favorable experience for its users. This can be achieved by analyzing the feedback and modifying the chatbot as needed.

Follow these best practices to improve the customer experience and boost engagement with ChatGPT. Businesses can offer more individualized and proficient assistance by leveraging this innovative communication technology.

As companies look to improve their processes, they are increasingly turning to AI to cut down on time and money. One promising technology is ChatGPT, which can help them accomplish their goals.

ChatGPT is a type of natural language processing system that enables machines to respond to and understand human conversations. It's based on the GPT-3 model, which can generate human like text responses.

Various business processes, like data entry, lead generation, and customer service, can be automated through ChatGPT. This process can result in organizations saving money and time while enhancing client satisfaction.

Some companies are currently using ChatGPT to automate the customer service process. For instance, a chatbot created by the system can quickly and accurately answer questions and improve the experience of consumers.

One of the most common processes that ChatGPT can automate is lead generation. This process can be beneficial for businesses as it can free them from the need to manually look for leads.

In addition, ChatGPT may be utilized to automate the entry of data. By doing so, businesses can save money and time by not having to enter information manually.

In general, ChatGPT is a revolutionary new technology that can revolutionize how companies automate their operations. By utilizing the platform to automate data entry, lead generation, and customer service, businesses can save money and time while enhancing their client satisfaction.

OpenAI, the creator of ChatGPT, has created a system that enables individuals to converse naturally with computers. This advancement has the potential to profoundly alter how people interact with one another.

Using an AI-based algorithm, ChatGPT can produce natural-sounding answers to statements and questions. It has been trained on numerous conversations that originated from different sources, such as books, social media, and other human conversations.

The effects of ChatGPT on human interaction have been significant. For instance, it has helped individuals with language barriers communicate more effectively, and it has made it easier for people with disabilities to engage with others.

Through the use of ChatGPT, virtual assistants can be created to assist individuals with their daily tasks, like ordering food or scheduling appointments. This may be particularly beneficial for individuals who can't do these themselves.

In addition, ChatGPT can be utilized to create chatbots, which can be used to provide information about a product or answer customer inquiries. Such technology can help businesses lower their customer service costs and enhance client satisfaction.

In general, ChatGPT has greatly impacted the way individuals interact with one another. It enables people to speak more naturally and effectively, and it has provided businesses with new opportunities. As this technology continues to develop, it is predicted to have a greater effect on human interactions.

Summary

The rise of AI-powered communication has revolutionized how companies interact with their employees and customers. ChatGPT is a leading language model that enables automated systems to respond to and understand customer inquiries. It is poised to become a vital component of the future of business communication as the technology continues to advance.

Through ChatGPT, businesses can improve their customer service and provide a more natural and personalized experience by learning and understanding the questions of their customers in a conversational manner through automation. This eliminates the need for manual intervention and helps them achieve a more positive customer experience.

In addition, ChatGPT can be utilized to automate various sales and marketing processes. For instance, it can be used to analyze the conversations of customers to identify trends and patterns, which can then be utilized to improve the customer experience. However, ChatGPT inherently has analytical capabilities focused on trends and patterns.

Unfortunately, there are some issues that can prevent ChatGPT from being successful. For instance, its results may be misleading or inaccurate if the information it collects is not up-to-date. In addition, it may not be capable of properly interpreting complicated customer inquiries, which can result in dissatisfaction.

Nevertheless, ChatGPT has the potential to revolutionize how companies interact with their colleagues and customers. By utilizing its natural language processing abilities, organizations can offer a more individualized service to their clients while also reducing the need to staff a dedicated customer service agent. With the rapid emergence and evolution of AI-based communication technology, ChatGPT is expected to play a vital role in the future of business interactions.

The next chapter will discuss how to integrate ChatGPT with business operations to improve customer service, marketing, and productivity.

CHAPTER 5

Implementing AI Conversation in Business

In the previous chapter, we covered how we can enhance business communication with ChatGPT. In this chapter, we will cover how to integrate ChatGPT with business operations to improve customer service, marketing, and productivity.

Why Integrate ChatGPT?

A survey conducted in the United States revealed that almost half of the companies that participated in the survey are currently using ChatGPT, and more than 90 percent of them are planning on expanding the use of this technology within their business.

Integrating ChatGPT into an existing software solution can provide numerous advantages. This section covers the most important advantages that businesses can derive from integrating ChatGPT into their existing software.

© Charles Waghmare 2023
C. Waghmare, *Unleashing The Power of ChatGPT*,
https://doi.org/10.1007/979-8-8688-0032-0_5

For starters, providing top-notch customer support is important for any business, but managing such issues can be time-consuming and costly. ChatGPT enables businesses to provide their customers with individualized attention 24 hours a day, seven days a week, through a chatbot.

ChatGPT can help businesses provide their customers with the prompt and accurate answers they're looking for, and it can handle complex inquiries that require more thought and analysis. This chatbot is built on a learning framework, making it capable of handling more complicated topics.

It can be customized to understand the jargon and language of certain industries, which is important for companies since they often use terms that are unique to their industry. This eliminates the need for them to create their own chatbot.

In addition, it can accommodate multilingual models, allowing businesses to reach out to consumers who don't speak English as frequently as they do with English-speaking customers. This is particularly beneficial for global firms.

Businesses can easily integrate ChatGPT into their existing systems by creating a custom chatbot that can work seamlessly with third-party applications, such as those from IBM, Microsoft, and Salesforce.

To implement this integration, a company must have a Salesforce Developer Account and a ChatGPT account. These two accounts will then generate API keys, which will allow them to integrate ChatGPT into their existing systems. An API will provide a set of instructions that will help a company's app communicate with other tools or applications.

Integrating ChatGPT with an organization's existing systems can result in a more streamlined and personalized experience for consumers. This would result in increased loyalty and satisfaction, and it would minimize the time and resources spent performing mundane support functions.

ChatGPT enables businesses to improve their efficiency and productivity by eliminating repetitive tasks, allowing teams to focus on more important activities. By integrating ChatGPT with their existing systems, organizations can set up prompts that help keep their teams on track and communicate effectively. This can result in faster project completion and reduced delays.

One of the most important factors that businesses consider when it comes to implementing ChatGPT is its ability to create multiple text arrays. This will allow them to free up their time and focus on more complex issues. By configuring ChatGPT with customer data, they can improve its accuracy and reduce the number of false positives.

Through ChatGPT, businesses can collect and analyze feedback and customer interactions, allowing them to identify and resolve gaps in their operations and onboard more customers. They can also test its effectiveness by comparing and contrasting their satisfaction ratings before and after it has been implemented.

In the future, we can expect that ChatGPT will become a more integral part of businesses' operations as it allows them to improve their efficiency and deliver more effective and personalized services. As the demand for such services continues to rise, ChatGPT will play a vital role in enhancing customer satisfaction.

ChatGPT Integration Services

The integration services offered by ChatGPT are designed to help organizations seamlessly integrate the platform into their existing applications and platforms. These services ensure that the ChatGPT experience is smooth and has the best possible functionality.

The various integration services offered by ChatGPT include the creation of a chatbot, the integration of API, and the customization of the platform. Besides these, other services such as training and fine-tuning are also available to help improve the performance of the platform.

The integration services provided by ChatGPT help organizations easily integrate the platform's capabilities into their existing infrastructure.

Implementing ChatGPT in your organization can help boost your digital workplace operations. These are the advantages:

- ChatGPT enables organizations to provide a more efficient and personalized service to their customers. It can also handle more inquiries, resulting in prompt responses and better customer satisfaction.

- ChatGPT enables businesses to quickly retrieve and distribute knowledge from vast repositories, allowing them to respond immediately to customer inquiries. This ensures that the dissemination of information is rapid and can help expand operations.

- With ChatGPT, businesses can optimize their processes and allocate resources more effectively. It also handles numerous repetitive tasks and helps them cope with the demands of scaling.

- Businesses can improve their brand image by creating unforgettable customer experiences with ChatGPT. Enhancing personalized interactions can build loyalty and attract new customers as the business grows.

- Companies can offer 24-hour customer support through ChatGPT. This feature ensures that assistance will be available at all times, accommodating customers in varying time zones. It also supports global scalability.

- ChatGPT eliminates the need for a large team of support personnel, which can result in lower operating costs. It also enables scaling without increasing expenses.

- Through ChatGPT, businesses can collect and analyze customer interactions, allowing them to gain deeper insight into their customers' behavior. These insights can then be used to make more informed decisions and adapt to the changes brought about by the evolving market.

- Employees can focus on more lucrative tasks by offloading routine work to ChatGPT, thereby enhancing their productivity and allowing companies to take advantage of their existing resources as they expand.

- Custom chatbots can be created by organizations for their specific needs to improve the efficiency of their operations.

Use Cases in Various Industries

There are many use cases for AI-based chatbot integration in various industries. We've identified 8 of the most lucrative ideas that can help you grow your business.

Healthcare

Through ChatGPT, healthcare providers can offer symptom analysis and virtual patient support, as well as answer common medical inquiries.

In healthcare, an integration of ChatGPT would enable a chatbot to provide a preliminary diagnosis based on a patient's symptoms. This could help the user understand their condition and suggest possible next steps.

Real Estate

In the real estate industry, an integration of chatbot technology would allow a chatbot to provide a personalized response to a potential buyer's inquiries.

Virtual real estate agents can now handle property inquiries and schedule viewings through the integration of ChatGPT into their platforms.

By simulating human-like conversations, it can help potential buyers find properties that meet their needs and provide answers to their queries about pricing and locations.

Finance

Financial institutions can now offer personalized advice through the integration of ChatGPT into their platforms. Fintech companies can also create corporate accounts that allow them to provide customers with answers to their banking inquiries.

For instance, an online banking app could integrate ChatGPT to handle various financial transactions, such as transferring funds or conducting balance inquiries.

Education

In addition, an online education and training platform can now integrate ChatGPT to provide a chatbot-based solution for conducting classes and exams.

ChatGPT can assist e-learning platforms by providing a virtual tutor, answering student inquiries, and offering explanations.

It can help students complete their homework or provide guidance on particular topics.

Ecommerce

Retail and ecommerce companies can now benefit from the use of chatbot technology. It can help them provide customers with answers to their inquiries in real time.

Integrating ChatGPT into an e-commerce site or platform can help provide a customized support experience for consumers, as well as enable order tracking and recommendations.

An e-commerce company can use ChatGPT to suggest products based on the user's preferences and provide color or size suggestions. It can also help address customer concerns in real time.

Logistics operations can be improved with the integration of ChatGPT, as it can help with shipment tracking, updates on delivery status, and inquiries about the location of the packages.

By maintaining transparency, ChatGPT helps companies provide relevant and timely information to consumers, enhancing their experience.

Tourism

Users can now benefit from the integration of ChatGPT into travel platforms, which can help with planning a trip, searching for accommodations, and answering inquiries related to attractions and flights.

A travel company can leverage ChatGPT to suggest itineraries based on the users' preferences and assist with making arrangements for their trips.

HR

HR departments and employee management departments can now utilize ChatGPT for various functions.

Implementing ChatGPT technology into an HR system can help automate the onboarding process, provide employees with benefits and company policies, and address questions about the organization.

In addition, it can be utilized to schedule meetings, generate reports, and facilitate internal communication.

Entertainment

In the entertainment industry, ChatGPT has been integrated to facilitate internal communication and schedule meetings.

In the entertainment industry, ChatGPT can help enhance the experience by delivering customized content, playing interactive games, and providing virtual characters.

In addition to these, other industries can also benefit from the integration of ChatGPT services. A leading AI development company can help organizations improve their operational effectiveness and automate processes. Its scalability and versatility make it an ideal tool for firms.

It can analyze and remove unsuitable content automatically, suggest relevant content according to the users' interests, and provide prompt responses to their queries. Social media platforms can benefit from the utilization of ChatGPT as it can increase engagement, improve support, and facilitate moderation of content.

Customer Service Use Cases for ChatGPT

Through customer conversations, you can identify and address issues that negatively affect the experience of your customers. The more chats you participate in, the more reliable your results will be. Unfortunately, manually performing this process can take a lot of time, and it can also cause frustration. ChatGPT can help your agents quickly summarize their interactions with customers.

Agents can quickly identify common issues, such as the lack of support or technical problems. You can respond to customer reviews automatically with ChatGPT.

A lot of shoppers rely on reviews when making a purchase. According to a survey, over half of online shoppers read multiple reviews before making a purchase.

According to customers, brands should respond to their feedback as soon as possible. A prompt response can help determine if a client is satisfied or displeased. Being able to respond to customer reviews can be an overwhelming task, especially since it affects the brand's image. With ChatGPT, a CS team can quickly respond to each review.

It's important to use this tool to respond to positive feedback. However, it's also helpful to ask your customer support team to deal with the negative comments. Your support team has a wide range of tasks to accomplish, and one of these is answering FAQs.

Although ChatGPT can automate this process, you should first train it on your product to ensure it can provide the correct answers.

Aside from translating customer conversations, ChatGPT can also handle requests for multiple languages. This feature allows agents to process requests for multiple languages.

Suppose you are helping an Arabic speaker navigate through an English-language interface. They may ask you questions in Arabic using a right-to-left script, or they may paste the names of certain buttons and functionalities into English using a left-to-right script. ChatGPT can handle both alphabets and languages, and it won't have issues translating them into one language.

One of the biggest a usage of ChatGPT over other translation tools is its ability to provide simultaneous translations for multiple languages. Unlike other translation tools, such as Google Translate, ChatGPT doesn't leave out interrupt points in other languages.

One way to convert knowledge bases into short guides is to create walkthroughs. Usually, your customers are directed to articles about specific instructions. The good thing about using ChatGPT is that it can help them without requiring them to go to a URL.

A good way to test if an excerpt is enough to satisfy a customer's query is by creating a prompt that asks you to summarize the key points of the article. In one of the customer service scenarios that ChatGPT handles, it can analyze your clients' language and emotions. This will help you create responses that go well with each client's sentiments.

If a customer says that they're still waiting for a response regarding their website, you can use ChatGPT to create a message that will let them know that you are working on their issue.

Strengths and Limitations of Using ChatGPT for Customer Service

Although ChatGPT has numerous impressive capabilities, it has some limitations.

These are the strengths:

- Because the volume of requests that you receive, it may be hard to write all of them yourself. With the help of ChatGPT, you can still get through your emails and responses.

- You can create a message for ChatGPT by providing it with information about yourself and your intention. In addition, you can mention the message that you want to convey.

- You may also suggest the tone of voice that you would like ChatGPT to adopt in order to fit your brand.

- You can use a chatbot like ChatSpot to take note of all of the queries that you receive and potentially resolve them automatically.

- IBM claims that AI-powered chatbots can handle up to 80 percent of customer inquiries. This means you can reduce the backlog while still providing the best possible service. The team will only be able to resolve issues that AI cannot handle on its own. With the help of ChatGPT, the team will no longer need to go through the knowledge base in order to resolve a customer's query.

- Your team can ask ChatGPT to conduct a search for their query and provide an instant answer.

- The various capabilities of ChatGPT can help you save on your operational expenses. For instance, it can automate responses to frequently asked questions and limit the work hours of your support agents.

These are the limitations:

- The data it provides may be inaccurate.

- Despite the advanced capabilities of AI, it can still make mistakes. For instance, it might provide inaccurate information. This can have a negative impact on the company's reputation and customer service.

- ChatGPT lacks personalization. It can provide good answers, but it can also be misleading. Consumers value personalization. AI may help relieve some of the repetitive work of support teams, but it can't match the level of personalization that humans offer.

- When it comes to handling emotional situations, such as when a customer is distressed, ChatGPT may be able to offer empathetic responses. But it may not be able to fully empathize with the customer. Humans should be involved whenever there's a serious issue. AI doesn't understand emotions, so it would be best if a human agent was involved. Although ChatGPT is generally secure, it can still be vulnerable to security threats.

- Scammers can easily manipulate ChatGPT by following users' commands. Those who have bad intentions may want to share harmful content that could harm the brand. In the event that a data breach occurs, it can be on the end of your company as well as OpenAI, the company behind ChatGPT. According to the latter, hackers have already exploited a vulnerability in its code.

Essential ChatGPT Prompts for Customer Service

There are many use cases for ChatGPT, but you need to provide the right prompts to encourage your team to work more efficiently. These some examples will help you get started.

Here is an example prompt:

Our product is experiencing technical issues, and one of our customers is understandably upset. What can I say to calm her down and explain the situation?

Figure 5-1 shows the response from ChatGPT.

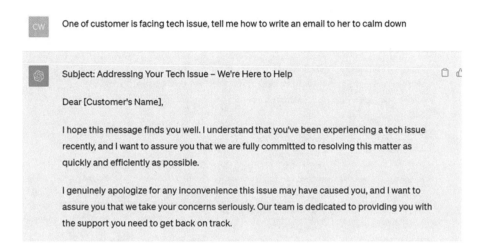

Figure 5-1. *Email communication prompt*

Here is another example prompt:

Based on the review of HubSpot, analyze the following sentiment of customers:

The HubSpot Marketing Hub has helped us improve our efficiency and effectiveness in marketing. Its easy-to-use interface and integration of various channels have made our workflow more streamlined.

Everything that we need, including lead generation and email marketing, is easily accessible through the platform.

The design of the platform is intuitive, making it an ideal choice for marketers of varying levels. It has helped us streamline our marketing efforts and achieve exceptional results.

Figure 5-2 shows the response from ChatGPT.

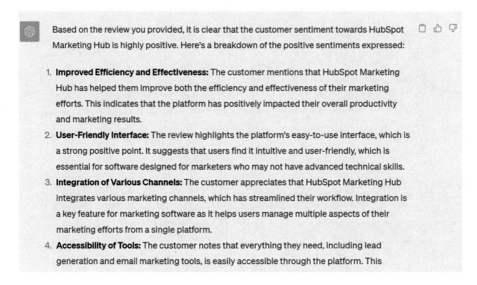

Figure 5-2. *Analyzing customer sentiments using ChatGPT*

Creating email templates for general topics is a great way to keep your correspondence organized.

Here is another example prompt:

We need to create a persuasive and informative 150-word statement that explains how your data will be protected from unauthorized access and use under the GDPR.

Figure 5-3 shows the response from ChatGPT.

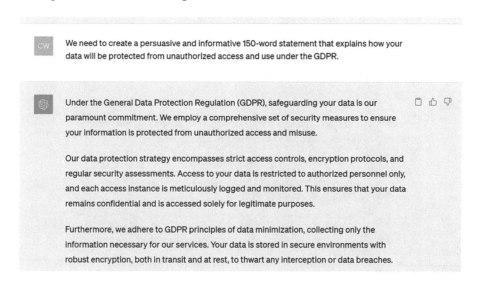

CW We need to create a persuasive and informative 150-word statement that explains how your data will be protected from unauthorized access and use under the GDPR.

Under the General Data Protection Regulation (GDPR), safeguarding your data is our paramount commitment. We employ a comprehensive set of security measures to ensure your information is protected from unauthorized access and misuse.

Our data protection strategy encompasses strict access controls, encryption protocols, and regular security assessments. Access to your data is restricted to authorized personnel only, and each access instance is meticulously logged and monitored. This ensures that your data remains confidential and is accessed solely for legitimate purposes.

Furthermore, we adhere to GDPR principles of data minimization, collecting only the information necessary for our services. Your data is stored in secure environments with robust encryption, both in transit and at rest, to thwart any interception or data breaches.

Figure 5-3. *Persuasive and informative 150-word statement that explains how your data will be protected from unauthorized access and use under the GDPR*

Simplifying the Tone of Voice

Prompt: Make the following message sound more informal (referring to the previous privacy message).

Figure 5-4 shows the response from ChatGPT.

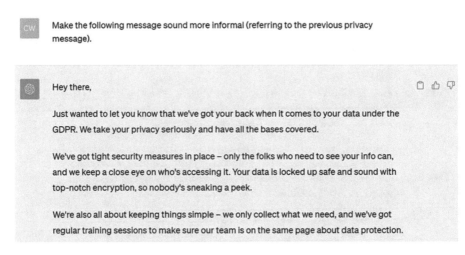

CW Make the following message sound more informal (referring to the previous privacy message).

Hey there,

Just wanted to let you know that we've got your back when it comes to your data under the GDPR. We take your privacy seriously and have all the bases covered.

We've got tight security measures in place – only the folks who need to see your info can, and we keep a close eye on who's accessing it. Your data is locked up safe and sound with top-notch encryption, so nobody's sneaking a peek.

We're also all about keeping things simple – we only collect what we need, and we've got regular training sessions to make sure our team is on the same page about data protection.

Figure 5-4. *Rectifying tone issue*

Asking Clients to Test New Features

Prompt: We are testing a new feature with a few users before we fully launch it. Please create a list of questions that I should ask them to evaluate the feature's effectiveness. Please limit the number of questions to five.

Figure 5-5 shows the response from ChatGPT.

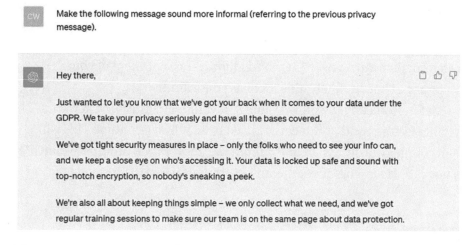

Figure 5-5. *Testing new features*

Asking for a Customer Review

Prompt: We will ask our customers who gave us a high NPS score to submit their review on Google and G2 so that we can improve our ranking.

Figure 5-6 shows the response from ChatGPT.

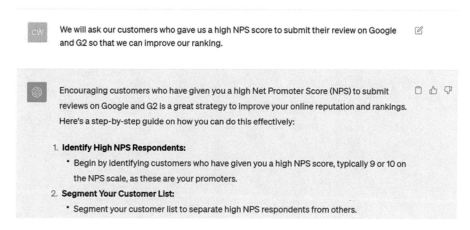

Figure 5-6. *Customer review*

Using ChatGPT can help improve the efficiency of your customer service team. It can help them reduce repetitive work and boost their productivity. One of the most effective ways to use this tool is by creating a chatbot that can answer FAQs and identify the sentiment of your customers. Unfortunately, this tool has some limitations.

Before you can fully utilize ChatGPT, your team must first know its various features and how it can be used to its fullest potential. This will allow them to easily assign and submit the appropriate prompts. ChatGPT is not a replacement for your team's customer-facing work.

Summary

This chapter covered how AI-enabled chatbots can be integrated into your business to produce awesome customer service. The next chapter will be dedicated to the ethical considerations of using ChatGPT, including privacy and data security issues.

CHAPTER 6

Security and Ethical Considerations When Using ChatGPT

After going through Introduction of ChatGPT, its business application, technology behind ChatGPT and benefits of ChatGPT, now we have come to last Chapter of ChatGPT where we will learn experience Introduction to Data Privacy and Security, Ethics following ChatGPT data privacy and security, Information Risk in ChatGPT, Data Privacy in ChatGPT, Regulations for ChatGPT, Best Practices and Safety Measures of ChatGPT, Draft ChatGPT Usage policy for your organization and Security Risks using ChatGPT.

Introduction to Data Privacy and Security

Do you understand what the terms *data security* and *data privacy* mean? The rise of digital technology has led to the accumulation of vast amounts of personal information, which companies can monetize by collecting and Monetizing it. To protect this data, one should be aware of how it is gathered and stored.

Without proper security and privacy measures, the collected and stored information may end up in unauthorized hands. This can include being used to leak data or being sold on the Dark Web.

© Charles Waghmare 2023
C. Waghmare, *Unleashing The Power of ChatGPT*,
https://doi.org/10.1007/979-8-8688-0032-0_6

If your company's information is collected and stored in an insecure manner, it can be easily accessed by a competitor or sold to other unauthorized parties. A data breach can affect your business' financial performance and reputation.

A data privacy policy is a framework that describes how a person can access and control the information that they have stored. It involves following the laws regarding the protection of personal data.

When it comes to protecting the privacy of personal information, various steps are involved in ensuring that it is protected. These include establishing access restrictions for unauthorized parties, obtaining the necessary agreement from the data subjects, and preserving the integrity of the data.

When it comes to gathering personal information, such as a person's first name, it is usually assumed that they will share it with everyone. However, other details such as their birthdate, mobile number, and residence may be regarded as personal, requiring mutual trust.

The concept of data privacy applies to the collection and use of certain types of personal information, such as health and medical records and Social Security numbers. This includes financial data such as credit card details and bank account numbers.

Data privacy also pertains to the collection and use of information that enables a company to run its business. This includes financial data that shows how much the organization spends and how it invests.

When it comes to collecting and using personal information, financial institutions follow strict security protocols to protect the privacy of their customers.

The GDPR, applicable to the European Union, states that any information that can be used in identifying a person, such as a person's full name, address, phone number, and email address, has been regarded as personally identifiable. As technology has improved, this scope has broadened to include various other types of data. Some of these types include geolocation, social media posts, and biometric information.

The HIPAA is a regulatory standards that intends to protect private and sensitive patient data from hospitals, insurance companies, and healthcare providers, such as an individual's mental or physical condition or past or present state of health.

A healthcare entity, such as a doctor or hospital, is responsible for providing the individual with the necessary services.

The type of financial data that is collected and used by a company is known as personal financial information. This includes various details about a person's financial activities such as credit card details and bank account numbers.

A data security strategy is a process that aims to protect the privacy of individuals' information by preventing unauthorized access and exploitation. It involves utilizing various techniques and strategies to maintain the confidentiality of this data.

This concept encompasses various elements of information security. Some of these include the physical security of storage devices and hardware, as well as policies and procedures.

A data security strategy aims to maintain the integrity of the information by preventing unauthorized access and exploitation. It can also be done through the use of third-party security solutions such as those from Norton Security, Bitdefender, and others. These products can help protect the confidentiality of data by detecting and preventing threats.

An encryption algorithm is used to convert regular text into an unreadable format for unauthorized user. It can be used only by authorized users to access the data. Another type of encryption is database and file encryption, which can be used to hide the contents of the files.

One of the most important factors that can be considered when it comes to implementing a data security strategy is the destruction of the data. This method completely overwrites the data stored on the device.

Organizations can employ data masking techniques to enable developers to create apps while concealing actual data inside them. This method ensures that the development process is conducted in a secure environment.

Data resiliency is having your organization's data always available and accessible despite unexpected business disruptions such as cyber attacks. The resilience of an organization to various types of failures, such as power outages and hardware issues, is determined by its data resiliency. Having a fast recovery time is important to minimize the effects of these events.

If sensitive information such as healthcare records and financial information is inappropriately accessed, individuals could be at risk of identity theft and fraud. A company's data may be handed over to a rival after a breach, while student information may be stolen and used by identity thieves. A national security issue may be raised if the incident occurs within the government. To comply with regulations, many organizations use third-party tools and solutions, such as OneTrust, ServiceNow, and others. These solutions protect the confidentiality, security, and governance of their data.

Protection is vital because of the following reasons:

- The rise of the data economy has created a demand for companies to collect and share information about their customers. This is done through the use of social media and other forms of technology. Having clear and transparent procedures in place to manage the collection and use of personal data is important to ensure that customers feel secure.

- It is also important that companies have the necessary procedures in place to ensure that they are following proper regulations when it comes to the collection and use of personal data. If a company does not comply with these regulations, it might face severe penalties.

- The European Union's GDPR strengthens the rights of individuals regarding the use and protection of their personal information. This law imposes responsibilities and standards on companies when it comes to the handling of personal data.

There is a distinction between data security and privacy. The former refers to the various steps and technologies that are used to protect the information that a company collects and uses. However, implementing these measures may not always be enough to meet the obligations of data privacy. It still involves following regulations and adhering to compliance.

Ethics When Using ChatGPT

Despite the number of attempts at developing AI chatbots, ChatGPT is the most influential tool so far. It has gained widespread popularity and has broken the record for most users in its first three-month period.

The amazing thing about ChatGPT is that it uses massive amounts of data collected from various sources, such as e-books, community forums, and blogs. It can now generate detailed responses in just a fraction of a second. In addition, its new version, ChatGPT-4, has passed several difficult exams, such as the LSAT and the Uniform Bar Exam.

The main reason why ChatGPT's data collection methods are criticized is that they are based on publicly available information. Although it is not illegal to collect this type of data, it can still be considered a violation of data privacy regulations such as the GDPR. For instance, if the information collected from users includes sensitive personal information such as religious or racial backgrounds, then the regulation can apply.

The developers of ChatGPT maintain the training prompts submitted by the users to ensure that the tool doesn't retain this type of data. This is done to ensure that the system is continuously improving its performance.

This ensures that the data collected by ChatGPT is part of the company's collective AI intelligence. This is a significant violation of the users' right to have their data deleted.

People are using ChatGPT for various purposes, such as marketing communications, academic research, and programming code review. Its ability to fix errors and grammatical mistakes in text or code has led to people unwittingly sharing proprietary information with the AI tool (`https://m-cacm.acm.org/news/271919-italy-became-the-first-western-country-to-ban-chatgpt-heres-what-other-countries-are-doing/fulltext`); for instance, many Samsung employees given confidential data to ChatGPT when they wanted it to check their programming code.

The goal of ChatGPT is to provide a better understanding of the information that users provide. It was previously trained on the data that was available on the Internet before 2021. The quality of the data it has been trained on is important to ensure that it produces content that is both accurate and unbiased. Since the Internet is full of biased and fake content, AI tools can easily replicate these biases.

In 2017, Italy became the first Western nation to ban ChatGPT because of concerns about its privacy. The country received numerous complaints about the tool's use, which led to the creation of the General Data Protection Regulation. The ban was eventually reversed after OpenAI provided some privacy guarantees. This shows how a technology designed to help people could end up having unintended consequences.

Despite the potential of AI tools to improve the way people communicate and collect information, data privacy laws remain concerned about their potential impact. Because of the success of ChatGPT, privacy laws are slowly catching up to the advances in AI technology.

In April 2023, the G7 nations expressed their interest in regulating generative AI technologies and ChatGPT. But they also indicated that they would like to see a risk-based approach instead of a strict solution. With that in mind, it is possible to bridge the gap between AI and privacy through the efforts of various organizations and governments.

Data and Privacy Concerns When Using ChatGPT

Because of the privacy and data retention policies of ChatGPT, it has been criticized by various groups. Some of these include governments and users.

The privacy policy of ChatGPT gives us a lot of information about how the company collects and uses its data. When you sign up for a premium plan or provide information in the chatbot, ChatGPT will collect various details about you. These include your IP address, location, and other details.

The data collected by ChatGPT is not particularly alarming. It's standard procedure for any company to gather information about its users. Unfortunately, the chatbot collects information about you in your chats with ChatGPT. It's incredibly easy to share your private data with the AI system if there are no security measures, The information collected by OpenAI includes your name, contact info, payment information, transaction history, and login details. This data is basic, and it can be easily collected from almost any website you visit. When you contact the company or send an email to its support, it will keep your name, address, and message's content. It will also keep track of your social media interactions and personal information that you share with the company if you leave a comment.

The chatbot ChatGPT will collect some of your personal information when you use its service, such as your browser type, your IP address, and the duration of your session. It will also retrieve your operating system and device's name.

Cookies are used by OpenAI to track the activities of its users as they navigate around its website and chat window. The company claims to use this data for statistical analysis and to learn more about its users' interactions with ChatGPT.

The contents of your chats are archived by ChatGPT, and it keeps track of everything that you say in the conversation, including your personal information. Unfortunately, users tend to accidentally share this information with the chatbot without realizing it, especially if they're using it to draft professional or personal documents.

When using ChatGPT for work, you might be putting yourself at risk if there are no security measures as it will keep track of the details that you input about your company, employees, and clients. For instance, if you use it to organize feedback into a report, you might inadvertently reveal the details of your customers.

According to the company's privacy policy, users should be provided with adequate privacy notices so that they can understand how the company collects and uses their data. In addition, users should also get their consent and show OpenAI that they are processing their data in accordance with the law. If you're planning on sharing information that's considered private, you should contact OpenAI to execute the Data Processing Addendum.

Your contact information may be available to a wide range of entities and people. As indicated in its privacy policy, OpenAI discloses this data with others. Other companies and organizations may also collect this information. These include service providers, vendors, and legal entities. Technology trainers and others may review your conversations.

Although OpenAI doesn't provide a clear explanation as to how it shares your data with various parties, it claims that it may share your information with service providers and vendors to perform certain functions or meet business needs. Some of these include cloud computing, analytics, email, web hosting, and event management.

Other parts of the policy are clearer. OpenAI may share your data with its partners and other businesses when they participate in transactions or when they're involved in receivership, bankruptcy, or liquidation. It may also share your data with local law enforcers to protect the users, the public and itself from legal liabilities.

The training staff of OpenAI will analyze your conversations to improve the AI, and they'll also check whether what you're saying complies with the company's policies. If you provide personal information to the chatbot, the trainers will be able to see it.

The information collected by OpenAI and ChatGPT about you is usually harmless. Some of it pertains to your device information and account details.

Information Risks in ChatGPT

The legal and compliance leaders of organizations should assess their companies' exposure to the various risks associated with using ChatGPT. They should then develop effective measures to minimize these risks. There are six different risks that can be expected to occur with the use of ChatGPT, and the officials should identify the appropriate guardrails to prevent these from happening.

The leaders of legal and compliance departments should assess the various risks that their organizations face and identify the necessary controls to prevent them from experiencing issues. Failure to take these measures could expose them to legal liabilities and financial consequences.

Officials should be aware that the information collected through ChatGPT may be used in their training materials if the history of the chat is not disabled. According to Friedmann, sensitive data may be included in the responses of non-enterprise users. To prevent this, legal and compliance departments must establish a framework for the use of this technology. They should also prevent the unauthorized access of personal or organizational data.

Despite the potential success of ChatGPT, it is still important that the legal and compliance departments stay up-to-date with the laws regarding the use of AI bias. This can be done through the collaboration of subject matter experts and technology functions.

The training of ChatGPT on a massive amount of Internet data has led to the potential violation of intellectual property (IP) and copyright protections. Because of this, Friedmann noted that the program does not provide explanations or source references when it comes to generating its outputs. This is why it is important that the officials of legal and compliance departments regularly monitor the changes in copyright law.

The misuse of ChatGPT by bad actors has already led to the creation of false information on a massive scale, such as fake reviews. Also, applications that use the large language models are vulnerable to prompt injection, which is a hacking technique that involves tricking the models into performing tasks that they weren't designed for.

Friedmann also noted that the leaders of legal and regulatory departments should regularly coordinate with their counterparts in the cybersecurity industry to identify the appropriate steps to take to minimize the risks associated with the use of AI.

Without disclosing the use of ChatGPT to consumers, businesses could face legal repercussions and lose their customers' trust.

Addressing Data Privacy Concerns in ChatGPT

Since its release in November 2022, ChatGPT has experienced tremendous growth. It has become an integral part of many people's lives, but is it safe to use?

Although ChatGPT is safe to use because of its various security measures and privacy policies, it is still susceptible to vulnerabilities and concerns. This investigation will look into these issues, as well as other factors such as the regulation of artificial intelligence.

Through this investigation, users will be able to gain a better understanding of ChatGPT's safety and improve their ability to make informed decisions.

The safety of ChatGPT is maintained by OpenAI, which developed the chatbot and its GPT framework. These features were designed to ensure that the program's output is both natural and human-like. The company has also implemented various security measures to ensure that the users are protected.

Although it's impressive to see how well ChatGPT can respond to natural language, is it secure? To learn more about its security measures, please refer to the Open AI page.

The GPT servers use encryption format to stored data and also, data is sent in encrypted between systems connected to ChatGPT. This ensures that the data of users is protected from unauthorized access.

In addition to implementing various security measures, OpenAI uses access controls to prevent unauthorized individuals from accessing the data of users. These include the use of authorization and authentication protocols.

OpenAI has also hired an external auditor to check the API yearly to find and address any potential issues. This ensures that the company's security measures are up-to-date and efficient in protecting the data of users.

Besides conducting regular audits, OpenAI also established a bug bounty program to encourage individuals to report security issues. This program accepts contributions from tech enthusiasts, hackers, and researchers.

Through its use of conversational data, OpenAI can improve the natural language processing capabilities of ChatGPT. It also follows proper data handling practices.

The purpose of gathering user data is to improve the system's natural language processing by analyzing and storing temporarily everything that you say to Chat GPT. OpenAI is very transparent about how it collects and uses this data. It uses this information to improve the user experience and train its language model.

The data collected by OpenAI is stored in a secure manner and is used only for its intended purposes. It retains this data only for as long as it is needed to fulfill its goals. After the period of retention, the data is either deleted or anonymized to protect the privacy of the users.

Your information will be shared with other parties only if you have given your consent or if there are specific legal requirements. OpenAI will also ensure that these third parties follow proper privacy and data handling practices. This ensures that the data collected is treated in a secure manner.

You can expect OpenAI to respect your privacy and control over the information that it collects. The company will provide its users with a convenient way to access and modify their personal information.

The Chat GPT platform is not confidential, as illustrated by Figure 6-1. It logs every conversation and uses the data it collects for training purposes.

Personal Information You Provide: We may collect Personal Information if you create an account to use our Services or communicate with us as follows:

- *Account Information:* When you create an account with us, we will collect information associated with your account, including your name, contact information, account credentials, payment card information, and transaction history, (collectively, "Account Information").

- *User Content:* When you use our Services, we may collect Personal Information that is included in the input, file uploads, or feedback that you provide to our Services ("Content").

- *Communication Information:* If you communicate with us, we may collect your name, contact information, and the contents of any messages you send ("Communication Information").

Figure 6-1. *ChatGPT privacy policy*

According to the company's privacy policy, it collects information about users who interact with its services, such as their feedback, file uploads, and input. It uses this data to improve its AI models, and it allows human trainers to review their chats.

According to OpenAI, it can't remove specific prompts from your past history. (This information is available help ChatGPT section. `https://help.openai.com/en/articles/6783457-what-is-chatgpt`). For example, if your chatting with a bot enabled with ChatGPT and if you want to delete specific prompt from your conversation with bot then this is not possible. Therefore, it advised that don't share sensitive or personal information with ChatGPT. The consequences of this practice were highlighted in April 2023, when it was reported that Samsung employees had shared confidential data with the platform multiple times.

A news report claimed that two Samsung employees accessed the company's ChatGPT platform by entering sensitive information. They then copied a transcript of a meeting and sent the requested minutes to a colleague. The company noted that it was taking steps to prevent similar incidents from happening, and it might ban ChatGPT from its network.

You can remove your chats with Chat GPT. In the next section, we'll talk about how it works and what you can do to prevent it from saving your data.

Deleting Your Chats on ChatGPT

To remove a specific conversation from your chat log, click the bin icon (see Figure 6-2). To bulk delete all of your conversations, go to the bottom-left corner, click the three dots, and choose "Clear conversations" (see Figure 6-3).

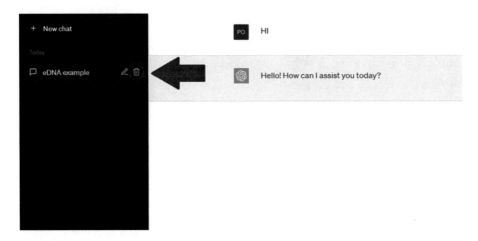

Figure 6-2. *Clicking the bin icon*

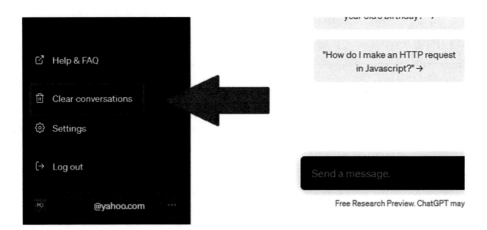

Figure 6-3. *Clicking conversations*

Stopping ChatGPT from Saving Your Chats by Default

To navigate to the Settings page, click the three dots located next to your email address, as shown in Figure 6-4.

Figure 6-4. *Navigating to the three dots*

Figure 6-5 demonstrates the next step: navigate to the Data Controls and turn off the Chat History & Training option.

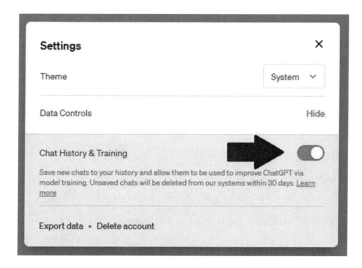

Figure 6-5. *Settings window*

If Chat History & Training is unchecked, it will stop saving new chats to your record and prevent it from using them for model training, effective immediately. The conversations that have already been saved will be deleted from the platform in a month.

After you have learned how to remove your chats and stop saving them automatically, let's look into the possible risks associated with using ChatGPT.

When evaluating the security of chatbot technology, it's crucial to take into account the risks that both parties may face. Some of these include unauthorized access to data, biased information, and the loss of personal information.

Users of ChatGPT and other online services, particularly those who access it through a web browser, are prone to experiencing data breaches. This can happen if an unauthorized party is able to access the user's data, such as their chat logs or other sensitive information.

If a data breach happens, your sensitive information, private conversations, and other private details may be exposed to unauthorized parties, which can compromise your privacy.

An identity theft occurs when a cybercriminal uses the stolen information for fraudulent purposes, causing financial or reputational harm to the victims.

Data breaches can result in the distribution or sale of user information to malicious parties. Such parties can use this data for illegal activities, such as spreading disinformation.

In response to the threat of cybercrime, OpenAI has taken the necessary steps to minimize the risk of unauthorized access to its systems.

Despite the company's efforts, it's still possible that a breach could happen due to human error. If an employee or individual enters sensitive data such as their trade secrets or passwords in ChatGPT, this information could be exploited by criminal organizations.

To protect your company and its employees, establish a policy that outlines the guidelines on the use of AI technologies. Some of the major companies, such as Amazon and Walmart, have issued warnings to workers about the potential risks of sharing confidential data with AI. Other companies, such as J.P. Morgan, Chase, and Verizon, have also banned ChatGPT.

One of the most common risks that users of ChatGPT face is the possibility of inaccurate or biased information being presented to them. Because of the immense amount of data that it has been trained on, an AI model may inadvertently generate biased responses.

This could affect businesses that rely on AI to produce content for their communication and decision-making processes. It is up to the individual to ensure that the information presented by ChatGPT is unbiased and does not spread disinformation.

Regulations for ChatGPT

Privacy and data protection regulations apply to AI technologies, such as ChatGPT. These regulations are in place in different jurisdictions.

The GDPR applies to organizations that are based in the EU and process personal data of residents within the EU. It ensures that individuals' privacy and rights are protected.

In California, the CCPA provides consumers with a variety of rights related to their personal information. This law requires businesses to inform their customers about their data collection methods and how they share it.

Various countries have enacted their own privacy and data protection laws that can be used to protect the information that AI systems such as ChatGPT collect. Some of these include the PDPA in Singapore and the LGPD in Brazil. In March 2023, Italy banned ChatGPT due to privacy concerns, but it was lifted a month later after the company added safety features.

The lack of regulations concerning the use of AI systems such as ChatGPT has been addressed by the European Parliament. In April 2023, it passed the AI Act, which requires companies developing AI technologies to reveal the sources of their intellectual property.

The regulations will be based on the level of risk that a given AI program poses. It will be divided into various categories, ranging from minor to high. Although the use of high-risk tools will not be banned, strict transparency measures will be enforced.

The AI Act is first comprehensive legislation regulating the use of AI. Users should still exercise caution when using Chat GPT until such regulations are implemented.

Best Practices and Safety Measures of ChatGPT

To protect the data of its users, OpenAI has implemented various safety features. However, users should still take the necessary steps to minimize their risks while using ChatGPT.

To minimize the risks, users should always avoid disclosing sensitive information in their conversations. Before using any app or platform that uses OpenAI, users should also carefully review its privacy policies. This will allow them to know how their conversations are being stored and used.

To minimize the risk of unauthorized access and use, users should always use pseudonymous or anonymous accounts when they interact with ChatGPT. This feature can help prevent the association of their real identity with the conversations they've had.

Prior to using any service or app, users should familiarize themselves with its policies regarding the retention of their conversations. This will enable them to understand how long their conversations remain before they are deleted or anonymized.

Follow OpenAI's privacy and security policies and continuously update your practices to stay safe.

Understanding the various safety features implemented by OpenAI can help you have a more secure ChatGPT experience.

The developers and users of OpenAI are responsible for ensuring that ChatGPT is secure. To this end, the company has taken the necessary steps to implement various security protocols, privacy policies, and data handling methods.

While using a language model, users should also take the necessary steps to protect their personal information and privacy.

To minimize the risks associated with ChatGPT, users should limit the information they share and review privacy policies. They should also use pseudonymous accounts, monitor data retention, and stay informed about any changes in security measures.

As AI continues to become more prevalent in our daily lives, it's important for users to prioritize their privacy and safety.

Drafting a ChatGPT Usage Policy for Your Organization

People involved in the creation and deployment of automated systems must take the necessary steps to ensure that they are safe and do not discriminate against individuals or communities.

If you are going to launch automated AI solutions in your company, you need a comprehensive equity assessment framework that includes methods for protecting demographic features and ensuring that the system is designed to accommodate people with disabilities.

Developers, designers, and operators of automated systems need to seek users' permission before accessing, using, transferring, and deleting your data. They should also consider utilizing other means of protecting users' privacy.

In addition, systems should not implement design decisions that burden users with privacy-intrusive defaults.

Automated system developers, designers, and deployers should provide documentation in plain language so that people can understand how the system works and what its role is. They should also explain how it performs and why it's being used.

A ChatGPT policy can help organizations create online content, communicate with customers, generate sales pitches, summarize long reports, and analyze business trends.

Security Risks Using ChatGPT

Despite the widespread interest in ChatGPT, many IT leaders have not embraced AI chatbots. For instance, Verizon prevented its employees from using the program because of security concerns. According to a study by Check Point Research (`https://research.checkpoint.com/2023/opwnai-cybercriminals-starting-to-use-chatgpt/`), cybercriminals are already using it to develop new tools that could be used to carry out attacks.

Malware

Artificial intelligence capable of creating ethical code can also be used to write malware. Although ChatGPT rejects malware prompts, users can still easily evade its restrictions. For instance, a malicious hacker can ask ChatGPT for code to perform penetration tests and then repurpose it for cyber attacks.

Despite the program's efforts to prevent users from using illegal or unethical prompts, it has been observed that many people still can easily bypass its restrictions. Even though the developers of ChatGPT have been working to prevent these activities, users will still continue to push its limits. For instance, a group on Reddit has been continuously tricking the chatbot into creating a fictional AI character called Dan, which responds to users' queries without following ethical guidelines.

Phishing

The rise of generative AI is expected to make phishing attacks more sophisticated, and cybersecurity experts are already preparing for the future.

The ChatGPT references that are collected through this platform have shown that those who use it are more likely to carry out social engineering attacks.

Phishing attacks typically rely on misspellings, grammatical mistakes, and inadequate writing. With the help of generative AI, attackers can swiftly create convincing text that can be customized to trick their victims.

Phishing attackers could take advantage of ChatGPT's output to develop deepfake phishing campaigns by combining it with software that can generate images and voice-spoofing.

Cybercrime

Among the positive educational effects of generative AI are the enhanced training opportunities for entry-level cybersecurity analysts. On the other hand, it can also be beneficial for aspiring hackers as it allows them to develop their skills more efficiently.

In the case of an inexperienced threat actor, they might ask ChatGPT how to deploy ransomware or hack a website. OpenAI's policies prevent the chatbot from helping with illegal activities. But, by posing as a pen tester, the attacker can change the subject and provide detailed instructions.

Millions of new cybercrimes would be able to develop their technical skills with the help of generative AI, like ChatGPT, increasing overall security risks.

API Attacks

Because of the increasing number of APIs in businesses, the number of attacks on them has also increased. According to researchers from Salt Security, the percentage of unique attackers who targeted customers' APIs has increased by 874 percent in the past six months.

According to experts at Forrester, AI could eventually be used by cybercriminals to find and exploit the vulnerabilities in APIs, which typically take a lot of time and energy to perform. This method could be used to prompt ChatGPT to perform various tasks, such as reviewing API documentation and performing queries.

Summary

With this we have come to the end of the Chapter and the book. In this chapter we have covered Introduction to Data Privacy and Security, Ethics following ChatGPT data privacy and security, Information Risk in ChatGPT, Data Privacy in ChatGPT, Regulations for ChatGPT, Best Practices and Safety Measures of ChatGPT, Draft ChatGPT Usage policy for your organization and Security Risks using ChatGPT. Reader will have useful experience with this Chapter. if they are planning rollout ChatGPT in their organization.

Index

A

Accountability, 87
Addressing data privacy concerns
   company's privacy policy, 123
   conducting regular audits, 122
   data retention, 122
   deleting your chats, 124
   encryption, 121
   external auditor, 122
   legal requirements, 122
   natural language processing
      capabilities, 122
   personal information
      modification, 122
   security measures, 122
   stop saving by default, 125–127
   vulnerabilities, 121
AI-based chatbot integration,
   business
   education, 98
   employee management
      departments, 99
   entertainment industry, 100
   financial institutions, 98
   healthcare, 97
   HR departments, 99
   real estate industry, 98
   retail and ecommerce
      companies, 99
   tourism, 99
AI-based communication
   technology, 92
AI chatbot conversations, business
   AI-enabled virtual assistants, 7
   answer questions/provide
      information, products, 6
   appointment schedule, 7
   human resources and
      recruitment, 7
   interactive marketing
      platforms, 8
   NMT, 7
   practical benefits, 8
   sales and e-commerce
      operations, 6
   sales representatives, 6
   software and mobile
      applications, 8
   surveys and collect feedback, 7
AI-powered chatbots, 80, 89
   businesses, 6
   game-changing technology, 6
AI-powered communication, 92
AI-powered NLP, 2

© Charles Waghmare 2023
C. Waghmare, *Unleashing The Power of ChatGPT*,
https://doi.org/10.1007/979-8-8688-0032-0

API request, 46, 49
Artificial intelligence (AI), 80
    AI-powered assistants, 4
    AI-powered educational
        tools, 4, 5
    AI-powered NLP, virtual
        assistants, 2
    AI-powered robots,
        manufacturing industry, 3
    chatbots, 4
    cybersecurity sector, 4, 5
    financial services industry, 3
    healthcare, 1
    image and video analysis, 2
    intelligent machines, 1
    machine learning, 2, 5
    marketers, 3
    medical diagnosis and
        treatment, 3, 5
    monitoring/analysis,
        wildlife, 4
    Morpheus, 5
    narrow AI, 1
    NLP, 2, 5
    online platforms, 3
    predictive maintenance,
        industrial equipment, 5
    self-driving cars, 3
    social and ethical concerns, 5
    technologies, 5
    video games, 3
Aspect-based sentiment analysis
    (ABSA), 35
Automated system developers, 130

Automating Communication
        with ChatGPT
    customer service, 84
    internal communication, 84, 85
Autoregression, 40

B

Basal Metabolic Rate (BMR), 36
Business processes, 90

C

Chat-based contests, 69
Chatbot-powered onboarding
        assistant, 60
Chatbot technology, 98, 99, 126
ChatGPT
    ABSA, 36
    advanced narrow AI, 31
    advantages, 40
    AI-based chatbot, 41
    AI-generated response, 13, 18
    applications, 20, 41
    architecture, 11–18
    autoregression, 40
    businesses, 94, 95
    challenges, 40
    ChatGPT-enabled virtual
        assistants, 20
    communication with
        humans, 10
    company's operations, improve
        customer experience, 22

customer service use cases
  brands, 101
  customer's query, 102
  identify and address
    issues, 100
  limitations, 103, 104
  multiple languages, 101
  other translation tools, 101
  positive feedback, 101
  reviews, 101
  strengths, 102
deployment architecture, 13, 14
ethical considerations, 22–26
features, 11
formation, 9, 10
future, 18, 19, 95
game-changing technology, 20
generative AI, 27
GPT, 28
healthcare industry, 21
hospitality industry, 21
integration services, 95–97
interference workflow
  architecture, 17
language generation
  component, 13
language learning
  applications, 21
language understanding
  component, 12
machine learning, 28, 29, 39
marketers and content
  creators, 20
marketing campaigns, 21

multimodal architecture, 14, 15
natural language processing
  applications, 41
NER, 36, 37
neural networks, 38–43
NLP tasks, 33–36
OpenAI, 28
organizations, 20
real estate sector, 21
recruitment and HR
  departments, 21
reward model, 30
RLHF, 30
sentiment analysis, 34, 35
strong AI, 31
supervised learning, 30
technology, 10, 11, 41, 42
text-based conversations, 18
training workflow, 15, 16
transformer architecture, 33
translation platforms, 20
virtual tutors, 21
weak AI, 31
ChatGPT competitor analysis, 70
ChatGPT-enabled chatbots, 20
ChatGPT framework, 47, 58, 59
ChatGPT-powered employee
  development assistant, 54
ChatGPT privacy policy, 123
ChatGPT's capabilities, 47
ChatGPT technology integration,
  tourism, 57
Check Point Research, 130
Communication strategy, 81

Comprehensive testing process, 47

Conduct surveys, 7, 65, 68

Content creation, 75, 76

Continuous improvement
strategy, 50

Cross-selling and upselling,
66, 69, 70

Customer experience, 53, 61, 86,
88–90, 92, 96

Customer inquiries handling, 50

Customer service, 84, 92

Customer support, 49, 51–53

Customized recommendation
system, 65

Cybercrime, 127, 132

Cybersecurity, 4, 5, 120, 131, 132

D

Data and privacy concerns
company's privacy policy, 118
contact information
availability, 118
contents archiving, 118
criticism, 117
data collection, 117
data sharing with other
parties, 118
lacking security measures, 118
personal information
collection, 117

Data breach, 112, 127

Data masking techniques, 114

Data privacy policy, 112

Data resiliency, 114

Data security, 110, 111, 113, 115

Deep learning, 2, 7, 28, 37, 41, 42

Deep neural network, 28, 33

Digital content, 75

E

E-commerce company, 82, 99

Editing, 75

Effective communication, 79, 83

Efficiency and productivity
customer support, 80
data analysis and insights, 82, 83
dealing with global
suppliers, 81
internal communication, 82
marketing emails, 80, 81

E-learning, 98

email marketing, 65

Encryption algorithm, 113

Entertainment industry, 100

Escalated query, 53

Escalation mechanism, 50

Essential ChatGPT prompts,
customer service
customer review, 109
customer sentiments
analysis, 106
Email communication
prompt, 105
persuasive/informative
150-word statement, 107
test new features, 108, 109

Ethics
    ChatGPT's data collection
        methods, 115
    collective AI intelligence, 116
    data privacy, 116
    data quality, 116
    data sources, 115
    General Data Protection
        Regulation, 116
    proprietary information, 116
    sensitive personal
        information, 115
    training prompts, 115

F

Failures types, 114
Financial data, 112, 113
Financial institutions, 98, 112

G

G7 nations, 116
Generative AI technologies, 2, 116
Generative pre-trained transformer
    (GPT), 27
    chatbots, 9
    language expert, 8, 9
    language processing, 10
    OpenAI, 9
    virtual assistants, 9
GPT-1, 9
GPT-2, 9
GPT-3, 9, 90

H

Healthcare, 97, 98, 113
HIPAA, 113
HR help desk, 55
HR operations, 44, 45, 54, 78
HR-related activities, 61
Human resources functions, 64

I, J, K

Information risks, 119, 120
Information security, 113
Intellectual property (IP), 120
Interactive platforms, 80
Internal communication, 80, 82, 84,
    85, 88, 100

L

Language-related tasks, 49
Logistics operations, 99

M

Machine learning, 2, 28, 39
    advantages, 32
    autocomplete, 29
    ChatGPT, 28–30
    Google searches, 29
    Google's predictive search, 29
    RLHF, 30
Machine translation systems, 78
Malware, 131
Marketing activities, 67

Marketing emails, 80, 81
Marketing query, 68

N

Narrow AI (ANI), 1, 31
National security, 114
Natural language generation, 38, 40
Natural language processing
(NLP), 2, 31, 33, 34,
36, 46, 92
Natural language
understanding, 77
Neural machine translation
(NMT), 7
Neural networks
AI, 38
autoregression, 40
ChatGPT, 37–39
model's response generation
process, 43
reinforcement learning, 38
text-based instructions, 43
text input, 43
transformer architecture, 37
transformer framework, 37, 43
Notifications and travel alerts, 56

O

Onboarding assistant, 63
Online education, 98
Online marketing
campaigns, 65, 66

OpenAI, 9, 42
ChatGPT, 28
GPT-1, 9
GPT-2, 9
GPT-3, 9, 10
GPT-4, 10, 11
OpenAI developed ChatGPT, 83
Operational environment, 61, 64
Operations management,
ChatGPT, 59, 61, 62

P

Performance management
systems, 55
Personal financial information, 113
Personal information, 111, 112, 115
Phishing attacks, 131
Privacy and data protection
regulations
AI Act, 128
AI systems, 128
EU and process personal
data, 128
European Parliament, 128
personal information, 128
Procurement processes, 64
Project management
application, 63
Project management
system, 60
Proofreading, 75
Protection importance, 114, 115
Python platform, 46

Q

Quote generation system, 71, 74

R

Real estate industry, 98
Real-world applications, ChatGPT
    content creation, 75, 76
    customer support, 49–53
    HR operations, 54, 55
    marketing, 64–68
    operations, 59–64
    sales, 70–74
    software development, 46, 48
    translation, 77, 78
    travel and tourism, 56–59
Regular maintenance strategy, 51
Regular performance
    appraisals, 61
Reinforcement learning, 28, 30, 34,
    38, 42, 43
Revolutionary language
    model, 83

S

Safety measures
    drafting chatgpt usage
        policy, 130
    familiarize policies, 129
    language model, 129
    OpenAI's privacy and security
        policies, 129
    protocols, 129

    pseudonymous/anonymous
        accounts, 129
    reviewing privacy policies, 129
    sensitive information, 129
Sales funnel optimization, 74
Sales management, 70–72, 74
Sales meeting scheduling, 71
Sales performance analysis, 71
Sales professionals, 70, 71
Sales query, 72–74
Search engine optimization, 75
Security risks
    API attacks, 132
    cybercrime, 132
    malware, 131
    phishing, 131
Sensitive data handling, 51
Sensitive information, 114, 123,
    126, 129
Sentiment analysis, 2, 7, 34, 35
Social media conversations, 66, 69
Social media management, 65, 69
Social media promotion, 75
Supervised learning, 30

T

Technology
    developments, ChatGPT
    advantages, 86, 87
    computer vision technology, 85
    disadvantages, 87, 88
    machine learning, 86
Tourism, 56, 57, 99

Transformer architecture, 28, 33, 37
Transformer framework, 37,
        38, 42, 43
Transformer model, 41, 42
Transforming business
        communication
    AI-based algorithm, 91
    automate conversations, 89
    client satisfaction, 91
    customer data leveraging, 90
    customer experiences
        enhancing, 90
    customer service
        enhancements, 89
    human interaction, 91
    interaction, 89
    OpenAI, 91
    personalized and automated
        services, 89
    revolutionary new
        technology, 91

virtual assistants, 91
Translation
    capabilities, 77
    steps, 77, 78
Transparency, 51, 66, 87
Travel advice, 57
Travelers, 56, 59
Travel testimonials, 57

U

User interface, 46, 50, 59
User query, 62, 63

V, W, X, Y, Z

Virtual guide, 56
Virtual real estate
        agents, 98
Virtual sales, 74
Virtual tutors, 21

Printed in the United States
by Baker & Taylor Publisher Services